BOLD
BRITISH
DESIGN

Hardie Grant

QUADRILLE

MODERN LIVING
SPACES TO INSPIRE
FEARLESSNESS AND
CREATIVITY

B

BRIT

DES

OLD

ISH

IGN

PHOTOGRAPHY BY SARAH HOGAN

WORDS & STYLED BY

EMILIO PIMENTEL-REID

INTRODUCTION

As a British citizen by choice, the idea for this book came from a desire to share the energy, inspiration and delight I have experienced in my roles as an editor, stylist and designer collaborating with the individuals I encounter in the UK's interiors world. Created in partnership with the talented photographer Sarah Hogan, *Bold British Design (BBD)* reveals a snapshot of UK design today by showcasing the houses and studios of 21 British-based people working in a range of interiors-related fields. Through profiles and short interviews we provide context and insight into their design choices. The various spaces reveal the distinctive elements of their work, personality, taste and training that leads them to create personal, stylish workplaces and homes.

Britain's history is woven through the narrative as creatives share their debt to designers of the past. From the technical virtuosity of Wedgwood founder Josiah Wedgwood's pioneering eighteenth-century ceramics manufacture to William Morris' (and the Arts and Crafts movement's) focus on craftsmanship in the nineteenth century, British innovators have since continued to propel design forward. Today creators the world over continue to admire British designers who combine heritage with wit, modernity and fun as they reinvent the elements of our interiors.

An understanding of the history behind today's design landscape should highlight retailers like Liberty (founded in 1875). Known for its printed textiles, the department store led the craze for Japanese and Indian craft as well as

working closely with designers promoting the then nascent Arts and Crafts and Art Nouveau movements. The furniture store Heal's, under the founder's great-grandson, Ambrose Heal, later led in innovation, combining good design with industrial production to supply well-made furniture to a broader audience. Both stores still continue to encourage and discover new talent and introduce the public to the latest in design. They were joined in the 1960s by Sir Terence Conran's democratic Habitat and the more upmarket The Conran Shop in the 1970s. Today, at a more rarefied level of the market, pioneering furniture and decorative objects are promoted by the David Gill Gallery, founded in 1987, one of the leading international galleries in contemporary design. Over the years the gallery has championed and collaborated with talent including the late internationally-renowned architect Zaha Hadid and award-winning David Chipperfield.

Looking towards other influences on British innovation the Festival of Britain national exhibition of 1951 promoted British design, architecture and the arts, paving the way for a contemporary and colourful post-war world. The exhibition influenced creativity in the years that followed and that period's aesthetic still attracts collectors of mid-century furniture to markets like Sunbury Antiques Market and the Midcentury Modern Vintage and Contemporary Interior Show.

It is relevant that this introduction was written in the double height library of the world's leading museum of applied and decorative arts and design – the Victoria and Albert

Museum (V&A) in London. With its origins in the Great Exhibition (1851) organised by the institution's first Director, Henry Cole, and Queen Victoria's consort Prince Albert, the V&A was created with the specific mission of enhancing industry and the applied arts. The vast collections, 145 galleries, exhibitions and archives continue to spark curiosity and inspire British creativity.

During the 1950s interior designers Nancy Lancaster and John Fowler began reinventing the past, creating the modern English country house look that is still channelled by lovers of traditional interiors. Not to be ignored are the bold influences of designers like David Hicks, known for his colour sense and love of graphic pattern (at his height of popularity in the 1970s), as well as David Mlinaric's connoisseurship of historic interiors and the great dealer–decorators, such as Geoffrey Bennison, Christopher Hodsoll and Christopher Gibbs.

And then there is the influence on young designers from the excellent schools – such as Central St Martin's and The Royal College of Art – that have trained many of the talented people you will read about in this book. British designers have an irreverent attitude to rules, which originates in the art schools' teaching – they encourage pupils to follow their instincts, resulting in the great freedom and originality that particularly characterises British design.

In today's interiors scene a respect for history coexists with extreme modernity. Craftsmanship and tradition are revered but not left to grow stale. International artistic influences blend with the home-grown, both as a result of media exposure and the arrival of immigrants who keep their traditions alive while becoming a part of our nation. It is in this context that the interiors and design we highlight here sit. The 21 individuals we showcase are by no means an exhaustive list of Britain's great talent pool; they have been chosen for the originality and boldness of their work as well as that of their interiors, and to higlight a breadth of styles and design categories.

The designers are bold, not just in the obvious sense of being colourful or quirky (as some gravitate towards muted palettes and their work is subtle) but they are all deeply original, fearless in their interior choices, either breaking the mould or pushing the boundaries of creativity. They are also bold in personal ways, often unconstrained by rules; joyful and courageous both in how an individual product is made or how disparate elements are bravely combined in a room. They also each exemplify many of the characteristics that make design in this country unique – a sense of humour and an appreciation for history, craft and modernity.

The interiors cover small and larger spaces and their owners make use of old and new, mass-produced and crafted products, colour and monochrome palettes. They range from the quietly refined to the eclectic with a hint of luxury; many break design rules and achieve inspiring results. While the designers have put great thought into their houses and flats, we have chosen to balance these by also showing studios for some. The workspaces give us an understanding into their design process while also helping to highlight the many product categories available in our industry and the immense thought that goes into creating these important elements of our home.

BBD is not meant as a 'how to' book or a guide to what to do in your home; it is more of a 'why not?'. Let yourself explore your own taste and creativity just like the designers featured. Our hope is that you feel emboldened by these personal insights to unleash your own story and creativity!

Emilio Pimentel-Reid

Collector and Antiques Dealer

GUY TOBIN

Realising early on that neither the army nor the unstable life of a practising sculptor were quite right, Guy Tobin joined an auction house at the lowest rung. Coming into contact with and handling objects in multiple sales week-in-week-out led him to a love and understanding of antique furniture. From there it was a short hop to the magnificent galleries of dealer Christopher Hodsoll where he further developed his connoisseurship over a period of 10 years. When Hodsoll closed, Guy went into partnership with another dealer with fathomless knowledge, Patrick Jefferson. Then, given the opportunity to join Rose Uniacke, a major tastemaker, Guy leapt to his current role as Head of Product. His eye and business sense have continued evolving while working alongside an interior designer with a deep sense of how a home should work and flow.

ATTRACTED BY THE POTENTIAL OF
WHAT HE COULD DO WITH IT, DEALER
GUY TOBIN SNAPPED UP A TURN-OF-
THE-LAST-CENTURY (1900) TERRACE
HOUSE IN LONDON'S BATTERSEA.
THERE WAS THE POSSIBILITY TO ADD
A TOP STOREY AND HE AND HIS WIFE
CELIA COULD EXPAND THE PROPERTY
OUT AT THE BACK. EVEN BETTER,
THE LOCATION WAS JUST RIGHT FOR
THE FAMILY. GUY WAS BROUGHT UP IN
SOUTH LONDON AND THIS HAS ALWAYS
BEEN HIS STOMPING GROUND.

Initially the brick house needed lots of work before someone as discerning as Guy could move in. Contemporary architects Hamish & Lyons were commissioned to reimagine the house as a more spacious incarnation. While the architectural practice is well known for its very contemporary projects, Guy's influence softened the hard lines of their modernity to create a pleasing balance. The collaboration resulted in a home where every inch is utilised and despite the fact that the house is not at all large it feels spacious and light.

On the ground floor of this three-storey house the transformation involved removing some walls to create a more open-plan layout, but the current placement of furniture creates defined zones. With this arrangement Guy has created a sense of elegance and formality that the house probably originally lacked, while avoiding the lack of clarity that can sometimes result from open-plan living.

In the entrance hall, to the right of the front door, a Semanier (a seven-drawer chest) by designer Rose Uniacke, flanked by Sri-Lankan ebony caned dining chairs, mingles with artwork by artists Pablo Bronstein and Celia's best friend, the talented artist Romily Hay. The round military concave lens injects fun and acts as a sort of circus mirror at the base of the stairs. 'The very best thing about British design,' Guy volunteers, 'as has historically

been the case, is our ability to draw upon the greater world around us. We may not be gracious enough to credit the initial inventor/ innovator but when we like something, we grab it as ours… perhaps with some adaptation.' Referring to the dining chairs: 'those chairs are a pure late Regency design made in Galle. They are an amalgam of local quality craftsmanship and English design.'

To the left of the front door the new plaster pendant light from Alexandra Robinson Design, inspired by a Chester Jones 1970s project, centres the living room area. Bespoke sofas upholstered in rich yellow and green Lelièvre velvets were created in just the right scale to fit the space.

The walls are painted in Farrow & Ball's 'Shaded White', a colour chosen to lighten the room which had been initially been a 'too-dark' green – a mistake that Guys acknowledges. Lots of table lights create flattering indirect lighting at night. The blue glass 1960s Italian mirror in the manner of Fontana Arte injects a touch of freshness.

The antique turtle carapace, a by-product after the turtle was eaten by nineteenth-century mariners, has been polished to create a lustrous white surface. The fireplace insert and the coffee table are in a rare vein of marble called Lumachella Antica, popular during the Renaissance, which enhances the feel of a collector's cabinet of curiosities with interesting natural objects gathered on a grand tour.

In the back living room, a Victorian desk – bought for a song at a local south London auction – turns out to be Gothic Revival probably by Charles Bevan, circa 1860s. Next to it the brass mechanical stool is raised by Guy's budding pianist daughter to play the keyboard and lowered by him to work at the desk.

Guy's kitchen incorporates stainless steel units and the design is in fact a functional statement of intent – 'I love cooking and I love restaurant kitchens,' he says. The choice of material subconsciously expresses that in this restaurant-style kitchen you will enjoy professional-style food. The polished slate counter top got stained immediately. 'I like the patina – it's the way things go,' he chuckles, and the use of monochrome abstract tiles from Fired Earth were inspired by a kitchen spotted in southern California.

In creating the kitchen space, 'we went back and sideways to expand the room's size as much as we could while retaining the small garden. The generous Arts and Crafts movement oak refectory table is surrounded by mid-nineteenth-century chairs with seats that I reupholstered in red leather. The antique table gets everyday use, has food and glitter spilled all over it and is the perfect height for making bread. It's a real workhorse piece of Cotswold craftsmanship.' By the doors to the garden a favourite chair and stool are also Arts and Crafts. The black cabinet glimpsed on the right wall was purchased at The Decorative Antiques & Textiles Fair and is Vienna Secession style.

Amongst all the antiques and art, Guy likes that his house, 'is a home: scruffy, comfortable, filled with bits and pieces that allow the eye to bounce about. It's endlessly changing, hopefully keeping my three young daughters on their toes and ever enquiring. Though they don't yet ask too many questions; they are not yet old enough (9, 7 and 2) to be taken by something. But they're surrounded by beautiful objects.'

For Celia the constant changing is probably her greatest source of fury. 'She is very involved in the interior,' adds Guy. Having worked for a well-known dealer her eye is as attuned as mine, particularly in fine art, but she is a little bit more neat and tidy and I'm more laissez-faire. We know that children may break something or rub their fingers on the velvet sofas. Luckily I am not a tyrant and neither is she. At home Celia's tends to focus on the art ensuring it's hung to its best effect. She has recently launched Pinxton & Co, a company that manufactures hooks.'

The children's bedrooms are on the first floor. The toddler sleeps in a mini art gallery featuring a collection of works. 'The big moth is by the wonderful Sarah Graham, a family friend and botanical artist who does everything on an enormous scale. The Regency Gillows mahogany chest of drawers works very well with our wall-mounted English Regency cabinet with its original wobbly glass which I've had for a long time. The oxen are from Sri Lanka – probably the second thing Celia and I bought together. They are Nandi bulls.'

The girls' room is next door. 'I have a firm rule with children, which is that I treat them as future adults from day one and so did not want a fluffy room for them. On the wall, the large-scale polar bear screen print is by Swedish artist Einar Hansen, dated 1932, which was bought on the birth of my eldest daughter. Instead of plush teddy bears, we have gone for gutsy animal elements. The painted fish shade on the bedside table lamp is by Romily Hay and is one of the special things she has done for us throughout the house.' In the context of artworks and antiques there is a nod to childhood in the duvet made from a re-edition of a 1930s fabric from Hollyhock Home.

The entire house has been put together with a collector's confidence. 'I never learned any decorating rules, so I fear I have no doubt broken them,' says Guy. 'My space came together as a cohesive accident. I've never been taught to do things properly and perhaps I just learned a lot by osmosis from the people around me. I was lucky that I lived for five years with my grandparents in a late Regency Gothic house in Shropshire while my parents were in South America. Their house was decorated by the eminent interior decorator

David Mlinaric known for his great flair for antiques and knowledge of historic interiors.'

'A personal rule which I don't think is taught at design school is the "sightline"; adds Guy. 'I love a caught glimpse or accidental view, through a door, down an enfilade, reflected in a mirror, the flash of greenery or sky.'

The serene bedroom, from which Guy catches these glimpses, includes personal touches like the white japanned lacquered table. It's an unusual piece, cream rather than the typical black, and also has sentimental attachment. It came from his grandparents' house, was left to his mother who absolutely loved it and then found a place in Guy's home.

Not unlike his objects and furniture, Guy has had an interesting trajectory. 'I started out being encouraged in the direction of the art schools as a fairly unruly 14-year-old,' he says. 'I think the choice was probably made for me with the help of an oxyacetylene blow torch and a brilliant sculpture teacher who introduced me to the work of Reg Butler, Twombly, Giacometti and Noguchi. Once I discovered the art trade via summer internships, I left the idea of physical making behind, in the hope of handling works by the masters. During the holidays I worked for a silver dealer at Portobello Road market. An introduction to the great art critic, David Sylvester, during my last year at school, and his rich yet sparse collection – one that crossed many disciplines – finally led me to the realisation that I wanted to be formed in the dealer–decorator mould. That of Geoffrey Bennison, Madeleine Castaing, Christopher Hodsoll or Rose Uniacke (the final two I have been lucky enough to work for).'

'When it comes to finding inspiration for my interiors and researching my purchases I have a pretty extensive library and use it daily. The collection of books grows weekly and covers all periods, nations, styles and subjects.

Perhaps the greatest source of creativity and stimulation for me is the result of falling down the research rabbit hole. I might be on a very specific hunt for the maker of a Wiener Werkstätte silver chess set and an hour later, surrounded by an encampment of books, I'll find myself looking at a medieval lancet window detail.' These happy accidents have led Guy in the direction of great erudition.

His style is 'driven by boundless curiosity and the stories behind the objects and their maker. It is acquisitive, fluid, ever-evolving and enquiring. The things I've bought recently range in period and design, including an eighteenth-century Sicilian side table, a nineteenth-century bust of Psyche and modern pot by Shiro Tsujimura. My preferences are less driven by a direction and more by the quality of the item. If I can attribute that thing to a maker or to an important school that makes things more exciting. I sometimes don't want to sell because each object I discover, buy and research becomes a part of me.' Craftsmanship and history are the primary drivers behind Guy's curiosity. Coming from an antique dealing background he is obsessive about the origin of everything, hence his library.

Looking to the future and where collecting is going, for Guy, 'it's more of a case of cycles of taste, either small tight circles over a few years or vast wheels over decades. Each (r)evolution just gathers a bit more tech, a few more 'names' and some arenas for dealers to introduce a new area for collecting.'

And how would the rest of us get started? 'Anyone with enough gumption to ask that question would need little help or advice. Those interested in such things as taste and personality, need to be curious, put their head down, listen, learn and deliberate with themselves and others, exhibit a degree of restraint and patience before just leaping in and having a go.'

'I never learned any
decorating rules,
so I fear I have no
doubt broken them.
My space came
together as a cohesive
accident.'

'I have a firm rule with children, which is that I treat them as future adults from day one and so I did not want a fluffy room for them.'

Illustrator and Painter

CAMILLA
PERKINS

'At home I could have
a bright Staffordshire
ceramic dog next to
a stern mid-century
armchair. I love the
juxtaposition between
the traditional and
the eccentric.'

Camilla Perkins derives inspiration from flora, fauna and everyday life, elevating her motifs with a dash of imagination to create highly patterned designs. As an illustrator she creates commercial work for advertising, as well as original paintings, prints, fabrics, designs for homewares and wallpapers. Since graduating from the University of Westminster in 2012 she has worked with various clients including Coca-Cola, Samsung and Anthropologie to produce brightly coloured and detailed images that channel a feeling of childlike wonder. Camilla was chosen as one of 2016's 'Selects' at the prestigious Pick Me Up illustration fair at Somerset House in London and has taught workshops at the V&A. She lives and works in Lewes in East Sussex.

HOW DO YOU DEFINE YOUR STYLE?

My style is bright, fun and feminine.

Those who like my designs are attracted by my use of colour and clashing patterns. I'm a 'textile head' inspired by textiles from different cultures. I'm attracted to Indian Kantha quilts, Asafo flags from Ghana – basically folk, outsider and naïve art with lots of colours and great typography.

At home I'm attracted to equally bright colour combinations. If I had it my way, I would live in a completely pattern-covered interior. My husband tones it down for me. He loves what I do and we share taste but I gravitate towards what I consider a 1970s granny vibe and he keeps it all under control.

WHAT SETS BRITISH DESIGN APART?

I think that British design means not being afraid to have a bit of fun with your style. Creatives in the UK have a certain eccentricity. Some of us like Victoriana and crazy pattern – there is a slight madness in the mix that somehow works.

At home I could have a bright Staffordshire ceramic dog next to a stern mid-century armchair. I love the juxtaposition between the traditional and the eccentric. In my living room I've pulled together a graphic pink painted lampshade on a vintage duck egg floor lamp from a car boot sale (both painted by me) with a velvet sofa and a bright yellow chair. My mum bought the deer antlers above the fireplace on eBay as a present for me 10 years ago.

I like to combine antique furniture and objects with more modern pieces though I do have to be more practical now that I have a baby. In Lewes they know me at the antiques shops and I use the baby's buggy to transport some of my finds.

ARE HISTORY AND CRAFTSMANSHIP IMPORTANT IN YOUR DESIGN WORK? HOW ABOUT TECHNOLOGY?

I'm really drawn to pattern and colour combinations from different cultures and periods throughout history. For example, I'm into Charleston (the Bloomsbury movement artist's house in East Sussex). I went to school down the road. When I was a child I would visit and come back home and paint all our furniture.

I wouldn't be able to function without technology as I mainly work digitally, though occasionally I have the time to get my paints out to create work, which is a process that I really love.

ARE THERE ANY DESIGN RULES ANYMORE?

Rules are made to be broken. I think you should just go for it. Sometimes the best work you make is from a spur of the moment idea. People can be very strict when it comes to colour combinations, but I like a more surreal approach; I like it when something is a bit weird. For example, the 'Power' poster on my staircase wall was made for an exhibition celebrating 100 years since women were granted the vote in the UK. I was heavily pregnant and had a uterus on my mind. I painted this very strong image influenced by anatomical illustrations. I added pattern to something that would normally be more academic-looking and made it fun and beautiful. I've since turned the original painting into a print which sold out on my online shop. In general, I would like to see people being more confident with introducing colour into their homes, even if it's just an interior door painted a gorgeous shade of pink – it can bring life to a room!

WHAT DO YOU MOST LIKE ABOUT YOUR HOME?

The fact that I finally have room to fill with things that I love. Coming from a tiny flat I can now hang my art and keep going.

I especially love the two blue pastels by British artist Hester Finch above the sofa, not just the colours but because her work feels so different to me. They really make this room special. I would not naturally put those colours together (blues and greens) but they work.

WHAT IS YOUR FAVOURITE ROOM AND WHY?

I love my daughter's room. Even though I have some really nice pops of colour throughout the whole house it's her room where I've been able to be the most playful with the design. I love her yellow fireplace. The pendant light I basically stole from my mother-in-law. It's art deco with a glass lamp shade with yellow, blue and green splodges. The print above the fireplace by me is called 'Breakfast in Santorini'. It's an illustration inspired by my honeymoon in Greece where I got pregnant.

WHAT MADE YOU WANT TO BECOME A DESIGNER?

When I was a child I went to an exhibition of Matisse's textiles and I left thinking that I wanted to make work that looked like that. I love illustration because you can literally work on anything – I could be doing character design for a commercial client one day and a pattern design for a fashion house the next. Illustrations can be applied to anything.

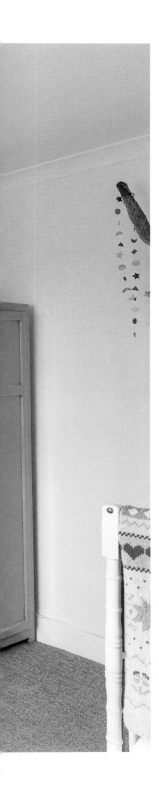

Ceramic Artist

HITOMI HOSONO

Japanese-born Hitomi Hosono studied ceramics at Kanazawa College of Art in Japan and Danmarks Designskole in Copenhagen before pursuing an MA in Ceramics and Glass at the Royal College of Art, London. She has been an Artist in Residence at Wedgwood. Inspired by nature and in particular the plants she discovers in east London, Hitomi explores and incorporates botanical details into her work, layering them to create her own visual language.

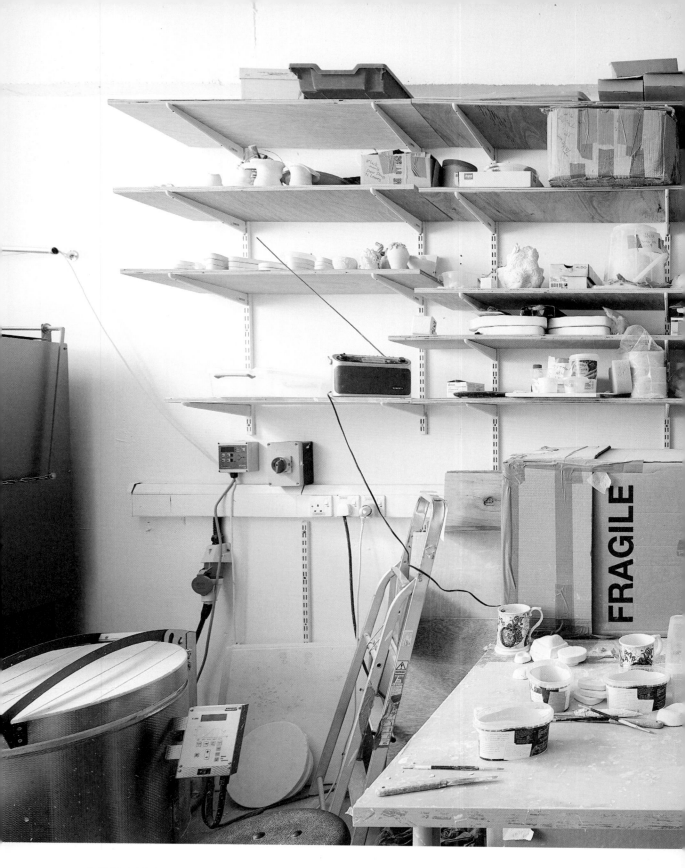

'My current ceramic work explores the beautiful shapes found in the natural world.'

IN A FORMER OFFICE BUILDING, NOW REBORN AS A CLUSTER OF THRIVING CREATIVE SPACES NEAR FINSBURY PARK, HITOMI HOSONO'S SMALL STUDIO IS FILLED WITH PROTECTIVE CASES MADE OF CARDBOARD AND COVERED IN CLEAR PLASTIC SHEETS.

Like stacked cocoons they protect something precious and delicate. This skyline of large boxes contains exquisite porcelain pieces quietly waiting to be dried – sometimes for a period of years – leaving little room to walk around. The gracious artist advises visitors to tread carefully among the clutter and fragility of her incubating creations.

'My studio has everything in one small room,' says Hitomi. 'This is the perfect size for me. I like that everything is at eye level.' A scan of the room reveals a large kiln, a potter's wheel and shelves of moulds and test pieces, the result of experiments mixing materials, as well as small random objects that Hitomi has collected simply out of curiosity. She sometimes visits these shelves to rediscover ideas or find a solution to a technical problem. 'When I walk around London I collect plants, like cherry blossoms in season, and I save them, along with objects that friends give to me, usually their own work and things we have swapped.' These collections reveal both the serendipitous nature and methodical approach to her craft, which is rooted in observing her surroundings, noticing the details, and exploring the properties of clay.

'My grandfather was a plaster worker who decorated walls with ceramic tiles. I am inspired by his work. I grew up in Mino,' she says referring to the Stoke-on-Trent of Japan, known for both industrial and hand-made pottery. 'Surrounded by all sorts of ceramics, I naturally became interested in designing ceramics myself.'

Hitomi moved to the UK from Copenhagen in 2007 to continue studying European ceramics. She chose Britain, lured by the Royal College of Art's ceramics and glass course's great reputation. 'I also wanted to learn more about British pottery like that produced by Wedgwood. It was my dream to challenge myself to develop new ceramic work while living within a city like London,' she says.

'My current ceramic work explores the beautiful shapes found in the natural world. I design leaf and flower sprigs by studying organic botanical forms in the garden, parks and streets, which I then adapt and interpret. I analyse plant forms by looking, touching and sketching. I am fascinated by the intricacy of plants and often examine how the veins of a leaf branch out and how its edges are shaped. I am always keen to find the essence of what makes leaves and flowers beautiful,' explains Hitomi.

The natural beauty found within plants inspires porcelain pieces with sensitively refined details. Favourite flowers such as the chrysanthemum, which reminds Hitomi of her hometown, often appear in her work. She is also fond of ferns and camellias. 'My family always used flowers for special occasions and I draw on these memories,' she says.

Living in the UK, Hitomi is often inspired by British architecture and traditional furniture. 'I look at ornament on buildings: the Natural History Museum in South Kensington is covered in beautiful details.' She also admires eighteenth- and nineteenth-century interiors and manor houses with their ornate ceilings, walls and friezes. 'I'm always discovering. Because I grew up in the East this is all new and I enjoy it.'

Hitomi's craft is grounded in historical methods. Her technique for making porcelain was initially inspired by Wedgwood's Jasperware, pioneered by founder Josiah Wedgwood over 200 years ago. This is the method in which thin ceramic reliefs or sprigs are applied as a surface decoration. 'This became a great influence. If I had not encountered this historical pottery methodology, perhaps I would not be making my current pieces,' says Hitomi.

'After the completion of original sprig models and the plaster moulds, I press-mould hundreds of leaf sprigs in porcelain and carefully and patiently carve the finer details. I then apply the porcelain leaves in layers on to a form thrown on a potter's wheel. I apply the leaves so densely that the underlying shape is entirely hidden, like a multitude of green leaves obscuring the branches of a tree.'

Reflecting on her work while hand-applying gold leaf to the inside of a box she reveals that craftsmanship is the most important element. 'I listen to the material – porcelain – in order to understand its limits and capabilities. I also continue to train my hands so that I can acquire further skills and learn new techniques,' she says.

Hitomi's much collected work doesn't just look backwards. 'In my mind, it is also very important for anyone working in design today to use the latest technology. When I was designing products for Wedgwood, I came to understand that technology makes the designing process much more efficient.' However, she points out that the 'combination of high-tech machinery and handcraft can deliver the best work'. At Wedgwood she remembers an experienced craftsman from her time as Artist in Residence who worked on a turning machine yet used his eye to identify and adjust imperfections that were too subtle for the machine to pick up.

'Innovation is one of the characteristics of British design. British designers consider how aesthetics and functionality can complement each other. They are also eager to respond to current issues, such as climate change, in order to influence our society'. Responding to climate change will influence design she believes. 'Design has often been all about mass production until now. The conversation has changed and consumers and collectors want better design and better materials. They want products and craft pieces that last longer. Handmade objects are more appreciated. Second-hand recycled furniture and decorations are more actively sought. This is coming from the awareness of environmental problems, such as global warming.'

An understanding of the past and present gives Hitomi's pieces a timeless quality and longevity. 'When it comes to style there are so many different trends around that I don't really focus on any. My work is about experimenting continuously. My material is always the same – clay, but I play with different textures and go on endless journeys. There is a lifetime of experimenting with this material as long as you are passionate and continue innovating. When clients buy my work, they of course like the flowers, the details, and the more they look the more they discover.'

'I listen to the material – porcelain – in order to understand its limits and capabilities.'

Pattern Designers

KEITH STEPHENSON AND MARK HAMPSHIRE

Based in Camberwell in south-east London, pattern designers Keith Stephenson, originally from Guisborough in North Yorkshire, and Mark Hampshire, from Leeds, launched their Mini Moderns interiors brand in 2006.

Having met while working at a graphic design agency and feeling that they weren't fully utilising their passions, they decided to do their own thing and be in control of their creativity. At the time Mark had previous experience as a product and furniture designer (his collection included cast resin mirrors, clocks and screen-printed cushions). Keith had previously been in fashion working as a print textiles designer. Sharing a lot of professional crossover, including knowledge about production, homewares made sense as a future endeavour to which they could apply their designs.

The couple, who are also life partners, specialise in designing pattern to apply across a range of products, including wallpapers, fabrics, cushions, rugs and ceramics. Their creations have developed a strong following from those who appreciate mid-century modern design with a contemporary twist. Their initial collection was snapped up by the influential Heal's shop and the brand continues to grow, selling online and via selected stockists around the world.

Their base is a modern townhouse designed to accommodate office space on the lower floors and a separate triplex apartment above topped by a penthouse living room.

HOW DO YOU DEFINE YOUR STYLE?

Mid-century modern-influenced with an appreciation of bold colour and pattern. If you look at our accessories we tend to go for graphic applied pattern. A lot of things around our home come from all over the place – contemporary pieces and objects we have collected growing up. Because we like junk shop finds we appreciate things that don't have a huge design pedigree. We've also made some furniture ourselves.

We got together because we shared a lot of things in common. Growing up as teenagers in the 1980s we were both obsessed with 1950s and 1960s design. At that time many of our friends would have a go at making clothes, for example, even if they just held together for one night. This is how we were introduced to the 1950s and 1960s printed fabrics we found at jumble sales. As we got older we started to recognise different designers, like ceramicist Susie Cooper, Portmeirion and Conran prints for Midwinter Pottery. We slowly developed an appreciation for mid-century modern, the design movement in interiors, product and graphic design and architecture that lasted from around 1933 to 1965.

WHAT SETS BRITISH DESIGN APART?

A spirit of adventure. When you look at some of the big furniture firms from other European countries, they are slick and there can sometimes be a sameness influenced by trends. In the UK we are less slavish to these tendencies. You can't really define a British look – it's idiosyncratic. We are more open to embracing the individual spirit and often incorporate a sense of humour.

British design pays attention to design history. You can often see designers paying homage to a design lineage, including great designers of even a century ago. We are influenced by people like textile designers Lucienne Day and Robert Stewart and also Terence Conran's pattern work before he founded Habitat, the retailer of household furnishings, in 1964.

ARE HISTORY AND CRAFTSMANSHIP IMPORTANT IN YOUR DESIGN WORK? HOW ABOUT TECHNOLOGY?

History most definitely is. Regarding craftsmanship and technology, we hand-draw all our wallpaper designs first then we re-draw them using Adobe Illustrator. Our wallpapers are produced using a traditional flexography method, which entails engraving the patterns on to rubber rollers and then printing them using traditional wallpaper machinery. All of the colours are mixed by eye by the colour technicians at the factory. You might go through many iterations before getting the colour just right. It's all an entirely visual process between us as the designers and the technicians who know their craft. Many are second-generation professionals keeping these skills alive. There is a sense of family and feeling for tradition. Our wallpaper designs are printed in the UK on FSC-certified substrate (paper) and we print with water-based ink.

ARE THERE ANY DESIGN RULES ANYMORE? IF YES, HOW DO YOU BREAK THEM?

We probably break wallpaper rules. We use subject matter for our wallpaper that isn't traditional. We are a bit maverick. The patterns that make up our designs are all personal: memories or motifs that reference our youth. We will channel everything from comic strips to tape cassettes or the Yorkshire landscape.

We only work with a palette of about 12 colours so earlier designs match our newest collections. This helps to give our work longevity.

WHAT DO YOU MOST LIKE ABOUT YOUR HOME ABOVE THE STUDIO SET UP?

The appeal of our building is that we can have the studio downstairs and lots of light and space in our home on the floors above. The house has adapted with us. As the collection has grown we can store and ship wallpaper from the studio, then go upstairs and escape it.

We constantly use the house as a creative resource; it's like a member of staff. We experiment and are always redecorating. Because of what we do the house naturally becomes a showcase for our work – whenever we design something new we can't wait to try it out.

We also do our own photoshoots and regularly have to buy props which we then incorporate into our interior. We make travel about work and pleasure.

We try to keep home and work separate though. The space is designed for that and we even have a separate front door to the studio. Our living room is three floors up from our work and above the study and bedrooms so you feel far enough away. Conveniently we can't hear the studio phone ringing when we are at home.

If you run your own business, zoning is important. There are areas for packing, then a control station for admin on the ground floor. We've had to really learn to separate our lives from work and had to be disciplined as we figured out how to live with the space.

WHAT IS YOUR FAVOURITE ROOM AND WHY?

Our living room on the top floor because it's open plan. Even though our building is a new build it feels like it's from the 1960s with an upside-down layout and great light.

We love our Robin Day 'Forum' sofa that we've had for a decade because it suits our aesthetic. It is not huge but generous in terms of seating and doesn't take up too much space. Our Scandinavian String shelving system is incredibly practical for storage and display opportunities. We've probably reconfigured it a dozen different ways. It even doubles up as a display on our stand when we exhibit at trade shows.

We collect very characterful ceramics and retro graphics and seek out the work of designers from the mid-century. A favourite is Alexander Girard whose whimsical work people think is targeted at children but it is not. On our shelves we love our commemorative glasses from the 1964 World's Fair in New York, which was conceived as a showcase of mid-twentieth-century American culture and technology.

We didn't know much about the fair when we bought them but being huge fans of the 1951 Festival of Britain (a national exhibition which took place in the UK) we were naturally intrigued by such a large scale exhibition of new products in the US.

WHAT ARE THE KEY ELEMENTS OF A MODERN, PERSONAL AND STYLISH INTERIOR?

A practical tip is to try not to be overly fashion-driven on the things you won't be updating, like tiles, or floors and taps. Experiment elsewhere, such as with wallpaper, paint or fabrics which are much easier to change. Create a neutral background and build from there. Plus you do not want to be wasteful with resources. Keep that in mind. Pursue your personal passions, whether that's objects you like to collect or plants.

HOW DO YOU SEE BRITISH DOMESTIC INTERIORS EVOLVING?

The biggest impact on British interiors is that more people are renting and living in smaller spaces – this influences how they decorate and what they invest in. The younger generation (our customer demographic), for example, focus on more temporary approaches to their interior decor. They will go for a punch of pattern with lampshades, bedding and adhesive window film. Cushions are another great way of updating a space without spending too much. That said, with new developments in wallpaper production, such as non-woven substrates, wallpaper is now far easier to put up and remove without a trace – so it has become a more viable option even for 'generation rent'.

'We constantly
use the house as a
creative resource;
it's like a member of
staff. We experiment
and are always
redecorating.'

BETHAN GRAY

Welsh-born Bethan Gray is one of the UK's most celebrated furniture and homeware designers. Bethan's ancestors went on an incredible journey across continents before settling in Wales and she has visited many of the places they passed through, inspired by a love of travel, art and culture. Today, her mission is to bring contemporary relevance to the traditional techniques from these regions – keeping both cultural narratives and craft skills alive. She believes in the power of telling stories through craft and design and has formed joint ventures based on mutual trust and respect that support over 400 highly-skilled craftspeople globally.

ON THE EDGE OF LONDON'S NOTTING HILL, OVERLOOKING THE GRAND UNION CANAL, IS BETHAN GRAY DESIGN, ESTABLISHED IN 2008.

The studio is comfortable, practical and tells a story about who Bethan is as a designer. 'I like to have my mood boards up on the wall and samples close to hand so that I am visually surrounded by what I'm working on,' she says. 'I'll put my research on to boards at the beginning of a project – maybe photographs of countries I've visited mixed in with images of interesting techniques and materials. I sometimes put actual samples up as my colours often come from natural materials. When projects have developed further, I put pictures up of the new product designs I have created and group them as a collection.' The walls become visual lists of all the pieces that Bethan and her team are working on.

'I've used calming colours and the windows open on to the canal, so there's a real connection with nature even though we're right in the middle of London. It's also lovely to be part of a community of creative practices in the surrounding studios,' says Bethan.

'I've brought my happy plants into the space – I'm a big gardener,' she confides. I love having plants around me, especially those with large leaves and a striking pattern. Swiss cheese plants make me very happy. We also take them to trade fairs so in a sense they are travelling plants. Plants are great for the air and they also create a cheerful environment to work in.

'My favourite corner at home has to be what my son has named my "cosy corner". We've got a gorgeous modular sofa that I designed so that it has plenty of space for everyone when we've got friends over but is equally cosy when it's just the three of us. It is filled with cushions and sheepskins and I love curling up there in front of the fire with a sketch book and a selection of my favourite frankincense or rose oil candles. In the summer it's the garden where we have lots of tropical plants. Even in the rain it's always green.' The studio channels this domestic sense of comfort while also serving as a busy creative hub.

Bethan grew up in a very creative environment and was always encouraged to pursue design. Both her parents have an interest in art. 'My father likes to paint and makes things out of wood. My grandfather was a forester and carved things for me. My mum always liked doing art and would make collages. I was always supported in my artistic pursuits as this was something that they enjoyed. Three-dimensional objects have always appealed to me, so when I did my foundation course after A-levels I knew I would specialise in something 3D. By the end of the course I knew I wanted to create functional objects, so furniture seemed like a natural choice.'

Her inspiration often comes from travel. 'My ancestors were a nomadic Rajasthani clan who migrated across Arabia and Persia over centuries before ending up in Wales where I grew up, so I think wanderlust is in my genes,' explains Bethan. I absolutely love learning about other cultures and always take thousands of photographs. Those pictures have become a visual reference library for my work. I also love spending time in nature and really enjoy the tactility of natural materials.

'My style is a combination of three things – bold, graphic patterns; a subtle palette of warm colours that I have spent many years refining; and lots of natural, tactile materials. My style comes from how I combine those things, often in ways you might not expect. In the 'Nizwa' cabinet the pattern is inspired by the fort of the same name in Oman. Some people think it has a Middle Eastern aesthetic and others think it's art deco.'

Everything Bethan does is about telling cultural stories through craft, so history and craftsmanship are a huge part of her practice. 'The starting point might be the billowing sails of traditional dhow boats, which inspired my 'Dhowi' collection of cabinets and are also used in the '1882' lustre collection, or the sunlight falling across the castellations of Nizwa fort, both of which captured my imagination on my travels.' She then collaborates with local master craftsmen to bring those stories to life. The studio embraces new technologies and often pairs cutting-edge manufacturing techniques with ancient handicraft skills. For example, the petals for the Nizwa cabinet are laser-cut, then assembled and inlaid by hand from 108 individual solid brass elements.

In Bethan's design world there are few rules. 'For me, it's more about capturing and communicating personal and cultural narratives.' Her 'Victoria' range for Italian brand Editions Milano was a marriage of two things: the traditional British ritual of drinking tea and classic Italian marble. For this collaboration Bethan cleverly combined her own culture and her client's. 'It all started at the V&A archive where I was inspired by a lot of the textures in the delicate tea sets from the collection. As the design of my products developed I went to see the craftspeople in Italy. By chance the collection had been hand-carved in Pietrasanta in northern Tuscany where I got married, so there was a lovely personal connection with the town and the makers. The final pieces, made of almost translucent Arabescato marble and warm, brushed brass are fun, modern and irreverent in a very British way.'

What, we ask, are the key elements of a modern, personal and stylish interior? 'The key word is personal. You've got to create interiors that suit your personality and make you feel comfortable. For me, that means strong patterns, calming colours and natural materials, ' says Bethan. One of her latest collections was developed incorporating

feathers and shells. 'People remember picking up and collecting both of these as children and they really respond to the materials.' She has used feathers that have been saved from landfill as well as abalone, capiz shell and pearl shell. These are all waste materials. 'Scallop shells are cut into pieces and coated with resin creating a very graphic pattern – the colours are amazing,' adds Bethan.

'In the UK we are creating very exciting work. I love the diversity of British design – its openness to new ideas and its global influences. My experience of growing up in Wales and living in London has been rich with cultural references from all over the world and I really value that.' Bethan speaks Welsh and considers herself part of a minority, which makes her aware of different cultures and open to their influence. 'When I travel I'm interested in differences. I also always try to link historical craft references into my work.'

She believes we'll see more and more craftsmanship in interiors. People increasingly want to tell their own stories and invest in furniture and accessories with real meaning – something they have a connection to. They want to know or have seen how an object was made, or have a connection to the material. 'Regarding my collection: customers are first attracted to the material, then they like the furniture and finally they respond positively to the fact that materials are sustainable.'

And what advice would she give someone wanting to bring out their own personality in their home? 'A lot of it is about having the confidence to buy what resonates with you and makes you feel good. Make a mood board to see how the things you like work together – and get hold of samples or see things in real life before buying. I'm very visual and like touching and feeling everything. Choose things that you have a connection with. There's no right or wrong; it's your home and you need to be comfortable in it.'

Designer and Entrepreneur

NICOLAS
ROOPE

Since graduating as a sculptor in 1994, Nicolas Roope has worked in a different field to fine art yet has always been drawn to thinking artistically – whether conceiving oversized retro phones or designing sculptural energy-saving light bulbs with Plumen. Nicolas does not respect a linear view of the world and instead chooses to blur boundaries between art and design and between creativity and technology. His intimate knowledge of digital culture provided his various enterprises, including Poke creative agency, Antirom creative collective and Plumen, with a unique approach to develope products, encourage fresh ideas and open new markets.

His work and designs have been recognised by some of the world's most coveted prizes and institutions. The first Plumen light bulb prototype was collected by New York's MoMA, and the Plumen 001 light bulb is also in the permanent collections of the Cooper Hewitt Smithsonian Design in New York, and the V&A and Design Museum in London.

HOW DO YOU DEFINE YOUR STYLE?

My style has a mid-century sensibility with a contemporary twist. You see it with my lighting designs where I create new bulbs that feel at home in retro interiors. Having studied sculpture, I create eye-catching beautiful objects that work inside shades and also within all the constraints of modern lamps. I aim to design practical objects but am aware of their potential to add visual interest to a lamp – beyond that of the commodified bulbs that they are replacing. They strike a balance and feel considered and harmonious.

My house in Highgate in north London is from the 1960s, an era I like because of its unfussy, basic construction, clear layout and lots of natural light. This is enhanced by great woodwork and decent materials as well as being generously proportioned with a garden at the back. The house is a simple geometric canvas. My home is modern while giving space for personality and feeling to come through. I like a simple canvas without being elaborate. Each room reflects different moments and makes sense for different activities. I keep it simple while making each space a pleasant place to be.

WHAT SETS BRITISH DESIGN APART?

British design is eclectic, quirky, sometimes grand, mixed with a blend of cultural influences. As a country our strength is storytelling and literature and we design more through stories than through just visual aesthetic. Our designs are the result of an intent not just a set of parameters.

All our Plumen bulbs have a very clear purpose, both functionally, but also in their desire to challenge the lighting industry in its narrow perspective on bulb design and the role of light sources in general.

ARE HISTORY AND CRAFTSMANSHIP IMPORTANT IN YOUR DESIGN WORK? HOW ABOUT TECHNOLOGY?

New technology drives what I do, but history shapes it.

Learning from the endeavours of the past helps inform the direction we should take with new technology, particularly when we are able to overcome problems insurmountable before. When we launched the 001, our most iconic bulb, technology limited performance. Now with LED we have better technology and have increased the lifetime, dimability, light quality and performance.

History has definitely influenced my work. One of my bulbs, the 003 (which I've used in my bedroom), is inspired by Danish lighting designer Poul Henningsen's sensibility. As part of the design process I explored the thinking behind Henningsen's PH5 lamp to create a bulb that uses direct and reflective light. The resulting 003 distributes light in a more efficient way than was previously possible.

ARE THERE ANY DESIGN RULES ANYMORE?

I don't think there are any useful rules, other than a general requirement to articulate and express ideas clearly and purposefully. This gives you an anchor in your rationale to achieve results.

WHAT IS YOUR FAVOURITE CORNER/ROOM AND WHY?

The dining room is my favourite space. I like spending time there and having people over. I used multiple pendant lamps and my 002 bulb, which is designed to be more mellow and not as bright. I needed more of them so that we could see our food, but this specific bulb also creates a special mood. The black shade kicks light back and is nice on the eyes, bathing faces in soft light without any glare. I also love the graphic arrangement the lights create.

HOW DO YOU SEE BRITISH DOMESTIC INTERIORS EVOLVING?

Interior style is globalising through social media and being increasingly influenced by restaurant, lounge and bar design. So it would seem that 'local' is losing its lustre. And yet with this come the perfect conditions for a backlash. With all trends you get tensions and the backlash is to move away from that – a counter-trend.

We're all trying to find our own identity in response to global style – the common language that seems to exist everywhere. There will be a move away from the trajectory where the whole world becomes uniform.

WHAT ADVICE WOULD YOU GIVE SOMEONE TO HELP THEM TO BRING OUT THEIR OWN TASTE AND PERSONALITY?

Design for you, not for the person you want to project as yourself. Try to play around and do not aim for perfection. On my dining room wall shelf, for example, I like to change things around. There are pictures of my parents and my wife's parents leaning against the wall and random pictures from a friend. I have a bit of memorabilia but nothing too heavy. There's a print of a church where we got married – the Danish Church in Regent's Park. It doesn't have to be complicated.

'We're all trying to find our own identity in response to global style – the common language that seems to exist everywhere. There will be a move away from the trajectory where the whole world becomes uniform.'

Interior Designer

GEORGIA COLLETT

Designer Georgia Collett was born and educated in London, studying fashion at Central Saint Martins and gaining a Masters in textile design at the Royal College of Art. For a number of years Georgia worked as a print designer for fashion companies including Orla Kiely and Alexander McQueen. In 2013 Georgia joined interior design practice Collett-Zarzycki where she has worked on luxury residential projects from London to Switzerland. Recently Christopher Farr launched a collection of her rug designs in collaboration with Collett-Zarzycki.

'Modernism seemed so out of reach to me when I was growing up, as the reality in London is often to live in a semi-detached house unless you build something modern yourself.'

PEDESTRIANS ONLY
NO
MOTORCYCLE
PARKING /
ACCESS
AT ANY TIME

ON A RAINY MORNING WE ASCEND TO THE TOP OF A MAGNIFICENT WHITE BRUTALIST BUILDING REMINISCENT OF A STEPPED PYRAMID.

The now iconic Alexandra Road estate in north-west London, fondly referred to as Rowley Way on account of its address, is a crescent-shaped structure of unpainted reinforced concrete. Designed in 1968 by local-council architect Neave Brown, it's the sort of visionary complex complete with school and urban parkland that is now being rediscovered by design-savvy city dwellers.

Georgia Collett's duplex, perched on the top floor, affords contrasting urban views across surrounding Camden, with railway tracks to the north and facing St John's Wood to the south, the lights from Lord's cricket ground and leafy Regent's Park in the distance.

At first glance, this upside-down council estate flat (the bedrooms are on the lower floor and the living room on the upper floor) is an unexpected choice of home for Georgia, a youthful creative force at her father's renowned interior design practice Collett-Zarzycki, who is used to applying her talents to conjuring luxurious interiors. 'I never thought I would find myself living in a mid-century design icon having only lived in Victorian and Edwardian houses. But here there is a real consideration for the best use of the relatively small space and so much light!' enthuses Georgia as she opens the door to her confidently eclectic space.

In the entrance hall a tall dragon tree plant fills the double height space and vintage airplane postcards are grouped and framed to create quirky wall art.

'Modernism seemed so out of reach to me when I was growing up, as the reality in London is often to live in a semi-detached house unless you build something modern yourself. Yet when I discovered this flat, I loved how it is so well designed, intelligent and different. It is human in scale and its use of space. Not a centimetre has been wasted,' says Georgia. Surprisingly it also feels very warm, a quality that is enhanced by the use of wood in the staircase, front windows, sliding panel frames and in the cabinetry throughout.

Injecting her strong appreciation of colour, pattern and tactile materials into this minimal space delivers an interior that is bold, restful, ordered and most of all comfortable. 'Comfort is one of the most important elements I considered. It's not just about having a squishy sofa, it's also about what surface you have under your feet and how easily one is able to move around the space.'

On the top floor, Georgia tackled the challenge of living in what is effectively one big room, creating order by defining spaces visually and having a place for everything. She has skilfully introduced visual interest, physical warmth and sensory comfort via her own rugs and textiles. 'My mother and father are both designers and I grew up in a very creative environment. I think my parents would have liked the idea of me becoming a lawyer but design was really the natural path for me. I'm more about creativity, aesthetics and problem solving!'

Her designs, in collaboration with Collett-Zarzycki for rug company Christopher Farr, now anchor several spaces, including 'Assembled Stripe', a low pile Afghan wool rug in the sitting area. The hand-knotted rug is made using an ancient technique that you don't see often and looks very modern. It is made in Afghanistan by a charity supporting local people, crafts and maintaining the tradition of rug-making in that part of the world. 'Craft is incredibly important to my design ethos. I think with manufacturing becoming more and more mass market and machine-led, it is the handmade and bespoke that are truly special and desirable. I feel fortunate to work with many small-scale British and international craftspeople in my work and it feels valuable to be supporting these artisans,' says Georgia.

In the flat, Georgia's bold rugs ground the pieces of furniture and also add sound insulation, warmth and tactility. 'Most of all they add supporting pattern in a room without feeling overwhelming, so that I can relax,' she says.

'My favourite spot is sitting on the sofa looking out of the huge south-facing windows and watching the sky change through the day.' The generous dusky pink two-seater sofa is sprinkled with cushions, including a red one in mohair woven by Georgia at art school. Behind it, sliding panel doors that close off the dining room display two prints of vases bought at the Maeght gallery in Paris. A Christian Astuguevieille 'Afridans' stool from Holly Hunt London playfully channels sunnier climes and a terracotta painted niche displays a portrait by a family friend, David Champion. The larger portrait, by Georgia's brother Jesse Collett, is given space to breathe and pops on the painted wall in a colour Georgia refers to as 'cement' and visually ties the room's palette together.

Around the corner, in the kitchen–dining room, tiles and cabinets have been restored to match the originals.

The 1960s dining table bought on eBay and chairs re-covered in new fabric look as if they've always been there.

In the main bedroom Georgia's own framed monoprint designs based on botanical drawings traverse the wall behind the bed, while there is a colourful crochet throw 'by my boyfriend David's mother', a pillow by Tibor on the bed, and fabric from her personal collection draped over the headboard. The silk rug, one of her own designs called 'Ink Stripe',

evolved from an abstract felt-tip artwork she created inspired by American quilts. The landscape painting on the bedside table was found at a house clearance sale.

Georgia shops everywhere, incorporating things that she likes with named and more expensive pieces. She confidently acknowledges the flat's history through her choice of contemporary furniture and accessories and layers of luxurious rugs, while whimsical pieces reflect her professional interests.

'British designers have an irreverent attitude to rules and are inherently creative thinkers,' she says. 'This has a lot to do with the fantastic art school tradition and the way young designers are taught to follow their instinct and develop a voice.'

This designer's style comes through sensitivity to materials, colour, proportion, symmetry and the property itself, creating an interior that is modern and stylish. In Georgia's own words: 'be confident, adventurous and trust your instinct. Don't take your home too seriously or worry about following trends.'

Sculptor

HAL
MESSEL

Hal Messel's work bridges the gap between silversmithing, art and sculpture. He is known for incorporating rare metals, crystals, shells and corals into his pieces and having trained in the traditional Huguenot silversmithing skills, Hal applies this knowledge to contemporary works of art. His style is whimsical and romantic.

Conveniently located at the centre of the buzzy market town is Hal Messel's Meeting House, a 1701 chapel – Nonconformist (later Methodist) and architecturally Victorianised – now resurrected as the sculptor's home, studio and workshop.

'It was derelict for 30 years,' says Hal, 'and needed rooms, floors, electricity, water... but otherwise,' he adds, 'it was structurally sound.'

Partnering with local architectural practice Millar + Howard Workshop, he has skilfully transformed the cavernous building into a logical and cosy space while preserving the magic of the chapel and the impressive ceiling height.

Creating a tall central raised platform, the architects have divided the nave into three clearly defined spaces: workshop, living room and kitchen, and have disguised the altar's high floor, which often destines similar conversions always to resemble a church. The resulting space feels sexy, loftlike and less ecclesiastical, with bedrooms, bathrooms and an office all discreetly hidden over two floors above the original entrance hall, allowing Hal to compartmentalise different aspects of his life.

'The joy of working to one's own desires and wishes is creating what you envisage,' he enthuses. The end result is roomy and filled with light: 'a place of peace and calm that creates the atmosphere in which to produce ideas.'

Considering the traffic intersection and bus stop outside, the Meeting House is oddly quiet. You can't hear the cars. The lower two windowpane tiers are frosted and from inside you can only see treetops, which transport you to the countryside.

Hal's favourite room is his workshop where he often finds himself getting lost in the reflections of the afternoon light shining through a stained-glass window. Although filled with machinery it is a place that produces an almost meditative approach to work. The space was designed as a contemplative place for an artist to create.

Messel studied fine-art oil painting at art school, and moved on to apprenticeships with Steve Wager and Jocelyn Burton in silversmithing. Designing pieces by hand in two dimensions, then making them and turning them into three-dimensional objects really fascinates him – the idea that if you can imagine it and draw it on paper, there will be a way of making it. 'I love working on commissions for clients, creating pieces that I know will be loved and cherished – hopefully for generations. Bringing light and joy to a room and creating an atmosphere of curious intrigue, stimulating fun and lively conversations. This is what attracted me to becoming a designer/maker and continues to motivate me.'

Enchanted by natural forms, the giant shells on Hal's work tables are prototypes for an exhibition at David Gill Gallery, one of the world's top design art galleries. 'Quite often my work starts by looking at nature and my environment, questioning how you would make that and how to interpret it in my own way,' explains Hal. 'I'm currently working on cutlery inspired by ferns unfurling to form handles. Nature always seems to get design right and as an artist I just add my own interpretation and voice.

'History and craftsmanship are also essential,' continues Hal, 'as they provide the vocabulary in order to understand how to create a great piece. At the same time, I think that technology should never be shunned. We are living in the Technological Revolution, which has many comparisons with the Industrial Revolution. The master of silver at that time was Paul Storr, who did not bemoan the "loss" of craftsmanship due to industrialisation. Instead he incorporated industrial processes into silversmithing. As a result, he innovated and produced work that stood the test of time. This is the approach I take, using technology as another tool in my toolbox.'

'We live in a really exciting time,' Hal enthuses, 'where anything goes. There is a freedom to create the unexpected. If it feels right and comes from personal inspiration it works no matter what. My clients also encourage me to push boundaries, giving me an opportunity to question why something must be a certain way. I see the future of British design becoming increasingly innovative while at the same time further developing an appreciation of skills and craft.

'In my work I try to apply this spirit of experimentation and innovation, incorporating unexpected large rough crystals, delicate and intricate coral, or polished concrete with silver. I always try not to design by convention but by feeling, although there are certain rules around geometry and proportion I tend to apply to my work as I find this creates harmony and rhythm. The Golden Section (a sense of proportion which is considered particularly pleasing to the eye) is key and is something that humans tend to utilise instinctively, being naturally drawn to its balanced aesthetic,' explains Hal.

'When it comes to creating my space, equally anything goes. If I think of my parents' generation and how they were faithful to a period – that approach to decorating is all gone. Personally, I'm interested in a mixture of styles, periods and materials, and particularly of texture and shape. There is however a theme and follow-through at home

so that there is cohesiveness; in the Meeting House I did this with colour.

'I feel that colour temperature is crucial. By having "cool" colour walls and "warm" colour floors and ceiling, or vice versa, you can create a dynamic backdrop, allowing pieces to "pop" within it. This also avoids spaces looking like porridge. Lighting is key: a mixture of uplighters, downlighters and a table or floor light can be the difference between a beautiful space lacking drama and atmosphere and it being a dramatic stage that evolves throughout the day.'

In the living room, several steps up from Hal's red-floored studio, the stunning 'Dad's credenza' by his father, furniture designer Thomas Messel, looks like something straight out of the Vatican. 'The trompe l'oeil green marble credenza is very much his style and was in fact made for my mother to store her paint materials,' explains Hal. Several portraits are by Oliver Messel, the celebrated artist and stage designer who was Hal's great uncle. Most were painted while he was living on Barbados and depict friends (including a 1960s Miss Barbados) and daughters of friends. The sectional sofa is split by an Ercol chair upholstered in cloth from Nomad Design.

'The griffin on the bookcase is a table-leg prototype for one of my father's designs.' Victorian family portraits and pictures that originally hung at the family's Nymans House add to the mix. The bookcase contains things Hal has collected that interest him, including African bronzes, crystal, fossilised wood and shells. A few breathtaking pieces within a simple setting deliver a space with tremendous depth, courage and style.

Several steps down, where once there was an altar, the kitchen is crowned with an overscaled red Moroccan light, bought to tie in with the stained-glass window. 'Something large and unexpected was needed; the space called for something contemporary and not churchy.' Although this is a traditional Moroccan design the thinking behind it is fresh and the context makes it work. The French cherry-wood vintner's table was bought in nearby Tetbury and displays Hal's coral and shell-inspired silver pieces. Dining chairs are by his father, who made an extra set inspired by a commission and then personalised them with a family crest.

Wandering back to the entrance hall and up a narrow staircase is when you first encounter the mezzanine level office/drawing room, the space where Hal draws. The red chairs were designed by his cousin Lord Snowdon (Princess Margaret's former husband) for the 1969 investiture of the Prince of Wales at Caernarfon Castle. A witch's ball spotted at a local auction house reflects the seventeenth-century Flemish tapestry, also from Nymans. The drawing table which gives the room its name belonged to Lord Snowdon and came from Kensington Palace. A large Victorian armchair pulls up to an oak refectory table and by not taking these grand pieces too seriously Hal manages to create a look that's casual.

The top floor contains two bedrooms and a living room. The summer bedroom is simply decorated with a brass bed and framed costume designs by Oliver Messel for the ballet Sleeping Beauty. Hal's sproodle, Mr Biggles, prefers the upstairs living room sofa to the layered rugs covering the floor. A portrait of fashion designer Carolina Herrera – also by Oliver Messel and one in a series, which she decided not to keep – adds a touch of New York celebrity and British quirkiness to the wall above a mahogany whatnot.

Commenting on British design, the sculptor believes we are very good at creating spaces that are practical, designed to be lived in and at the same time luxurious, full of character and charm.

And the trick to achieving such a pitch-perfect interior? 'Look with your eyes and heart and not with your ears. Do not be afraid about whether it may or may not be the "right" thing to be interested in, or that you may not have the knowledge to like it. Loving something cannot be dictated or learned. It is felt.

'I have found that collecting things has taught me a great deal. I am drawn to collect certain things, such as ancient Greek coins, as well as crystals and minerals. I don't have many but what I continue to learn from them is inexhaustible in terms of heartfelt understanding and appreciation.'

'In my work I try
to apply this spirit
of experimentation
and innovation,
incorporating
unexpected large
rough crystals,
delicate and intricate
coral, or polished
concrete with silver.'

let us kneel before the Lord our maker.

Designer Craftsman and Environmentalist

SEBASTIAN COX

Sebastian Cox is the founder and co-director of his eponymous company, together with his wife Brogan Cox. He trained in design, making and sustainability and works mostly in wood, overseeing a team of designers, craftspeople and timber enthusiasts at his studio and workshop in London.

Sebastian is often found running between the workshop and design studio next door, admiring and selecting boards of wood, drawing new and handsome ideas for furniture, fixing machines and passionately driving the business forward.

'Design goes beyond the aesthetic – it is something deeper. It comes down to solving problems. Right now, the biggest problem we are facing is protecting the planet.'

SEBASTIAN COX SHARES HIS STUDIO AND WORKSHOP WITH HIS CO–DIRECTOR AND WIFE BROGAN COX AND THEIR TEAM OF MAKERS.

Metres away from the River Thames in Greenwich, south-east London, it surprises many who visit that modern furniture manufacturing is still happening in the British capital. And it very much is here – with wood planks going in at the woodworking mill and sustainable contemporary pieces, often bespoke, coming out of the workshop at the other end.

The feel of the workshop is slightly traditional in an Arts and Crafts Movement sense in that pieces are being made by hand with a limited range of biodegradable and renewable materials. The 'Mycelium + Timber' light shades, for example, are grown from mycelium, effectively a fungus, on to green wood waste from Sebastian's woodland. The mycelium feeds on the freshly cut wood and binds it together as it grows, creating lightweight, strong and completely compostable pendants. The studio's 'Wealden' collection comprises richly-textured rural tableware pressed from Kentish clay between chestnut wood moulds. Leather and ancient grain are materials the studio have more recently started working with. Sebastian's bread baskets – 'Landrace' – are thatched from heritage wheat, as opposed to the chemically-grown wheat that leaves fields bereft of wildlife.

There is something radical as well in the way Sebastian and his team of youthful craftspeople use the past to design and make new pieces for the future. For one, Sebastian only uses British timber, some of it sourced from his own traditionally managed woodland in Kent.

Sebastian likes the feel of the business with its relaxed environment. 'I love the light, and all our workshops face south,' he says. 'It is full of warm people as I prioritise having individuals with shared values.' There are plants in the windows, tools, and machinery that aids, but does not replace, the maker.

'I became interested in design via making,' says Sebastian as we tour the workshop. 'I knew I wanted to create something with my hands and the way to have autonomy was to become a designer. To be a designer today I felt I had to learn about sustainability. Design goes beyond the aesthetic – it is something deeper. It comes down to solving problems. Right now, the biggest problem we are facing is protecting the planet. Aesthetic needs to come second, the priority is the way we use our resources. In my area of design, the pattern of creating seasonal collections is uncomfortable. It has become an endless cycle.

'I find inspiration in the problems that face the natural world,' continues Sebastian. I am attracted to projects that protect the natural habitat. Coppicing, the traditional method of periodically cutting back a tree to ground level, would be an example of this. It is a forgotten method of woodland management developed over thousands of years that boosts biodiversity and has a long heritage of craft, tools and ways of working.'

'When it comes to my style, I try to make our work as style-less as possible in order to extend its longevity. But bigger than a style there is something else happening at the moment,' Sebastian explains. 'We are a part of a movement where people are connecting to where things come from and are wanting to have something that is tangible and real. Styles come and go and we now seek to be part of something more permanent. Only time can judge whether we achieve that with our work'.

History informs the work Sebastian creates. He looks back at the past to learn about how we should be living now. 'We used to build complex societies from a selection of materials that could be returned to the earth. We need to learn how to live in an equally sustainable way again. This is something that's not new but something to re-learn. At the studio we look to the past not out of nostalgia and sentimentality, but out of a need to reconnect how we live with the natural world.'

When it comes to design rules, 'the number one rule is to think of the end of the life of a product. This leads you to design something that will last. It should be repairable and the designer must ensure that it grows old gracefully,' says Sebastian. 'We should be aware that as designers we have a duty to create products that don't damage the planet. We are the generation that will be responsible for what happens next.'

This responsibility to the planet incorporates enjoyment and practicality. In the studio the open-plan office is set up as a part-showroom, part-domestic space.

By the front door there's the 'Pendean' settle in English ash designed by Brogan as a place to put your coats, helmets and shoes. It's a favourite perch for Willow, the workshop dog belonging to the couple.

In another part of the studio a woven 'Bayleaf' settle made from English chestnut defines a cosy space for working at the large 'Bayleaf' table made from ebonised oak and London plane. The 'Barker' emerald occasional table represents a new direction for the studio, injecting colour into the collection, in this case using medieval pigment.

The collection's well-considered pieces are meant to be enjoyed and lived with. Sebastian believes the key elements to enhance one's interior are objects that have meaning. 'In order to create a material culture that has longevity, we need to put things in our homes that mean something to you. This meaning can also be about how objects are made and where they come from,' he says. 'The current British design industry is unique: emerging brands are more likely to make things themselves and craft is an inherent part of commercial design today. We don't have a very broad availability of manufacturers in the UK, so here the only way to realise the design is to make the pieces yourself. A problem has become an opportunity. Young businesses are making the most of that and new generations are forming their business around self-production.'

We finish our visit by having one last look at the studio which is curated by Brogan to showcase the collections of textural work in a calm and tranquil setting. It's a space that warmly welcomes visitors after their journey to or across London, allowing clients to settle in among the couple's work before and after a sensory tour of the workshop. This space encourages creative thought, discussions and design in an open and collaborative environment which very much captures the ethos of their brand.

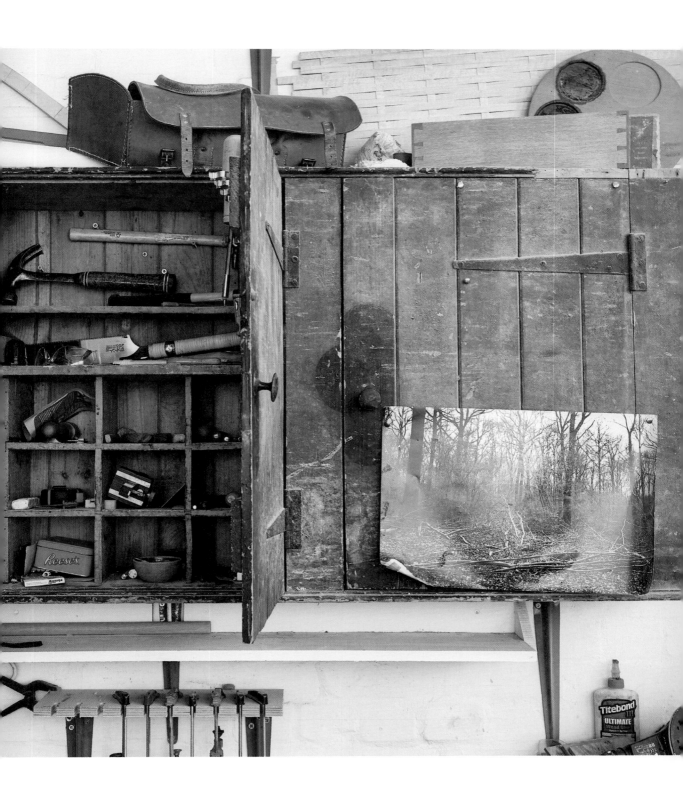

Designer

LIZZIE DESHAYES

Founding partners Lizzie Deshayes and Tim Butcher created Fromental with a mission to make the world's most beautiful hand-painted and hand-embroidered wallpapers, fabrics and accessories. Combining the finest skills with luxurious fabrics, their distinct style blends traditional high-end craftsmanship and artistry with a forward-thinking approach to design and creative techniques. Fromental offers contemporary, timeless interiors.

Lizzie takes great pride in reinventing aesthetics, adding a unique twist to chinoiserie designs and creating totally new wallpaper styles with traditional techniques. As Fromental's Design Director, she develops new hand-painted and hand-embroidered wallpapers, fabrics and accessories while constantly evolving the brand's signature style.

SEARCHING FOR NEW FROMENTAL OFFICES, DESIGN DIRECTOR LIZZIE DESHAYES AND CREATIVE AND PRODUCTION DIRECTOR TIM BUTCHER CHANCED UPON TWO SPACES ON THE SAME FLOOR OF A MODERN BUILDING IN QUEEN'S PARK, NORTH-WEST LONDON.

One now houses offices and the other, seen here, became a stylish showroom apartment that incorporates Lizzie's studio. This space, which looks like an indulgent and refined loft, showcases the Fromental wall coverings that sometimes entail artists spending up to 600 hours painting and stitching individual panels.

Lizzie abhors white walls; she finds them unsettling. Believing that a craftsman cannot work in a void, she craves the visual mess of books and objects; in short, the clutter that you encounter in a domestic space. The apartment is filled with precious objects that Lizzie wanted to have in her environment, plus some of the more boundary-pushing Fromental creations. 'We like to surround ourselves with the sorts of fabric and wallpapers we love and would like to make for others, as well as the colours we enjoy,' volunteers Lizzie while graciously serving us tea in the living room corner of the large space.

'It's not that often that we can sell some of the more unconventional designs,' she says, while surveying the surrounding open-plan room. 'This is the only place where we can have our complete vision for Fromental. Not everyone will choose to have bronze walls but we certainly can, and we use our space to tempt clients with all that is possible. To feel comfortable in a working environment is important. The plants, the antiques, the looms – I love all that surrounds me because a craftsman is not a craftsman in isolation.'

Lizzie carefully considered everything that went into the apartment and studio's interior, joking that she'd like to live at the V&A, but

as she couldn't she had to create her own inspiring space here.

Most of the stuff came from Lizzie and Tim's larger home and a lot from less grand sources. 'Wonderful brown furniture made by craftsmen is being thrown out,' laments Lizzie. 'There is beautiful product created today, but the hand of the maker has often been removed. I gravitate towards worn, loved, utilitarian pieces. A lot of our objects derived beauty from their utility. But I don't gather any old tat,' she clarifies. 'I would not pick up something that is too far gone or deteriorated; I prefer things that are in good nick and extremely well made.' The consummate hunter, she reveals, 'it was easier to find good pieces 10–15 years ago, but for those with a developed eye, a lot of nineteenth-century stuff is still kicking around.'

An Edwardian barley twist chair, perhaps a prayer chair, is going away to be upholstered by Lizzie's mother. She is an embroiderer and is making a needlepoint chair cover. There is also a beautiful Harris loom that was a gift from her godfather who is a weaver.

By a large window, vintage chairs and a wicker-topped table cosy up to one of the exquisite screens Fromental makes for clients. Handily, Lizzie's brother-in-law is a master cabinetmaker and he produced it with specially commissioned paper. The 'Nonsuch Bird' pattern in custom-coloured blood red on a gunmetal grey silk background is part-embroidered in a flat satin thread. The lucky bird perches on a branch, which is hand-painted and hand-embroidered creating a raised three-dimensional effect. The screen shows customers that there are many ways to use wallcovering. 'We're more than a wallpaper company; we make decorative objects and designs that can be applied to many wonderful surfaces and uses,' explains Lizzie.

Lizzie's favourite feature of the studio are the bookshelves. They remind her of her youth, when she had the luxury of owning her time exclusively and could spend hour upon hour reading and learning. 'Every moment I can, I open a book and it feels like stepping out of time.' The books are the most important possession she owns. 'If there were a fire I would burn because they are too precious to lose. My first expensive purchase was a book on the work of surrealist visual artist Man Ray. I worked hard, saved and bought it.' Lizzie is such a collector of books that every year a new bookshelf is built by a friend to accommodate her purchases. 'I'm happy when I close the studio door, sit on the floor and read.'

This collection of books is also a great source of inspiration and nurtures an interest in design which arose when she was young. Lizzie remembers being no more than five years old and precociously deciding she wanted to shape her environment to her own taste. 'A healthy disregard for any teacher telling me I should concentrate on their subject rather than my passion for drawing made it obvious fairly quickly that design would be my career,' Lizzie remembers. She was born in London to an English mother and French father and lived in France, where she was schooled until 17, then prepared her portfolio to study textile design in Britain.

Lizzie is proud to be a third-generation art student. Her grandmother attended the Bloomsbury Art School for Women and her mother studied at Camberwell and then Newcastle. 'Growing up I absorbed the aesthetic sense of John Allen, my godfather and textile designer. I picked a tapestry out several years ago and realised that he inspired what Fromental has become. He was such an influence from a young age. His approach to colour and the natural world made me who I am. My mother gave me the blessing to go to art school.

'I find inspiration absolutely everywhere and anywhere: from the cracks in the pavement,

to the detail in a medieval sculpture. 'Walking around in an ugly environment breeds guilt and guilt builds violence. Surroundings need to help with our mental well-being. I want to wake up feeling happy, in a space where everything belongs and everything belongs to me. That extends to my studio.'

'At Fromental we want to make people feel good with beautiful design crafted well. It would be ideal if more people could access beautiful design,' she acknowledges 'but craft is expensive. I wish there was less mediocrity and that some of the beauty filtered down to other purse sizes.'

On a studio wall above Lizzie's drawing table hangs an Uzbek gown with sleeves outstretched. As a source of inspiration, it fascinates because it combines Uzbeki Ikat and Russian print. The country of origin is situated on the Silk Route and you can see the provenance of the design. These gowns tell a tale of how cultures blend.

The painted snakes designs she is currently working on have always fascinated her. 'Les Boas' design mixes boas and pythons and will become part of the collection.

'I don't think I have a particular style,' says Lizzie. I am an avid collector of detail. I want to use and combine everything I find interesting and beautiful. Art, history and technology are the three pillars of our ethos at Fromental. As a totally design-led company, we try to be as knowledgeable as possible about the history of art and design, execute our work as well as possible and embrace all production methods to make the best decorative object possible.'

Lizzie often layers and combines various historical inspirations as part of her creative process. Every design she puts together comes from at least three different routes. First, a printed object or piece of fabric from the past. Another print or fabric will inspire the composition, and another source inspires the colour. Throughout the process she combines one element of inspiration with the other and sees if they can work together. The result will be unique; she will have created something new while acknowledging that she has taken from different sources. 'You can't hide the sources you're celebrating; in the same way that Cubism took from African art. We are all naïve when we think we've discovered something new. In my mind British design always has an eye on the past but plays a game with the viewer, challenging him or her to find out where the inspiration came from.'

At Fromental they use modern and traditional production methods. Following the Arts and Crafts principle Lizzie does not neglect any process and considers everything from embroidery to digital printing to hand-printing. At the studio she chooses a technique according to what is going to produce the best result for her design. 'We value them all the same as long as the result is beautiful. Everything is always hand-drawn and hand-made first. Technology sometimes allows us to play with hand-drawn elements to still produce a one-off design and for it to be economically viable. We don't waste; we make to order – we are not creating landfill.'

In the apartment the panoramic 'Shimla' landscape in the 'Phoenix' colourway is printed on handmade paper. The original design is entirely hand-painted in sections first, then scanned so that each element can be moved around and manipulated to fit a specific room. 'We can't customise like this with block print,' adds Lizzie. 'If a room has high ceilings, for example, we are able to recompose the design to fit the space. This is not meant as a shortcut; it is the right solution to a design problem.

'When it comes to design, I can't stand set rules; they are one person's imposition on another. Parameters on the other hand are wonderful; they allow a fiercer creativity. Boundaries help when we have to work to a certain budget. They focus your production methods. In the creative process clients are imposers of limits. We receive an inspiration image from a client and a colour palette. Sometimes you don't like what you've been given and then you have to create something beautiful within these constraints. For example,' says Lizzie, 'I may have to base my design on a photograph supplied by a client and I need it to be a panoramic wallpaper and only use hand-painting and silk screen. These guidelines force me to find the best solutions but with beauty.'

On a table that does double duty for meetings and dining, the 'Bruyère' wallpaper in the 'Weld' colourway was inspired by the work of Jean Lurçat, the French tapestry designer and artist. Lurçat devotees recently celebrated 100 years of his birth, and the artist's name came back to Lizzie, who has loved his work since she was a child.

On top of the panel sits a palette of silk colour samples that are available for embroiderers to use. They are hand-dyed in small batches and Lizzie's supplier has bound them into a little book so that she can communicate colour choices with clients and embroiderers. This illustrates the kind of bespoke design service that Fromental is able to offer.

With an eye to the future, Lizzie believes that 'design is moving towards a new appreciation of craft, and an awareness of waste will lead people to incorporate objects with longevity and eternal appeal into their homes rather than consuming blindly.'

'Live with the objects that appeal deeply to you and have a story of their own as well as those that relate to you,' she says. 'That way you are less likely to tire of them, and above all, don't give a damn what anyone else thinks.'

'We like to surround
ourselves with the
sorts of fabric and
wallpapers we love
and would like
to make for others,
as well as the colours
we enjoy.'

Artist and Designer

YINKA
ILORI

North-west-London-based designer Yinka Ilori specialises in upcycling vintage furniture inspired by the traditional Nigerian parables and African fabrics that surrounded him as a child. Having studied Furniture and Product Design at London Metropolitan University his work has been exhibited from Basel and Bilbao to Lagos and Stockholm. Humorous, provocative and fun, each piece he creates tells a story. Bringing Nigerian verbal traditions into playful conversation with contemporary design, Yinka's work touches on themes as diverse as hope, sexuality and social class.

Yinka is passionately against the unnecessary waste he has seen in European and West African consumer cultures and this drives him to reuse discarded furniture and other found objects. He is interested in playing with the relationship between function and form and his work sits between traditional divisions of art and design.

HOW DO YOU DEFINE YOUR STYLE?

My style is a combination of British and Nigerian heritage fused into furniture and interiors. The British side is more minimalist and relaxed. The Nigerian element is more flamboyant, inspired by everything from music to the clothes some Nigerians wear.

Minimalism to me is the opposite of what I saw growing up. I look at how my parents dressed and what they went to church in and they did not try to fit in. The attitude was: 'I know I'm going to get attention but I don't want to lose my culture.' In my view in the UK there is not that much colour in what people choose to wear.

The British element in my design comes through the type of furniture I create. The aesthetic and the shapes, which are very linear, clean and polished.

WHAT SETS BRITISH DESIGN APART?

British culture is not just one culture, it's a mixture of many. I'm first-generation British and I'm exposed to so many cultures in London. My work reflects the fact that I've been exposed to so much since birth.

ARE HISTORY AND CRAFTSMANSHIP IMPORTANT IN YOUR WORK? WHAT ABOUT TECHNOLOGY?

Both history and craftsmanship are important. If you look at Marcel Breuer's Bauhaus 'African Chair' you see that it was modern (in 1926), hand-carved and closely-inspired by African carving. Looking at a historic piece like that is a gateway to understanding the importance of both elements and then you move forward from it.

On a current project I'm using digital design to create, which allows me to work very quickly. There is so much you can do with colour, patterns and shapes and I can make mistakes, erase them and start again.

ARE THERE ANY DESIGN RULES ANYMORE?

There is no design rule book. We all create differently; my work is different from others. I like to make mistakes and don't seek perfection. My aim is to amplify the storytelling in my designs. All my chairs come from very personal places.

As an artist you give so much away – there will always be an element of my upbringing and background in my work. I stay true to myself by injecting colour in my projects. I use a lot of pink, lilac and yellow – that is my trademark palette. For me colour is about celebration and remembering a moment, and these colours remind me of a particular personal time. I put happiness into my work.

WHAT DO YOU MOST LIKE ABOUT YOUR STUDIO?

The fact that it is really colourful!

WHAT MADE YOU WANT TO BECOME A DESIGNER?

I don't really know. Growing up, anything creative was not respected because you didn't wear a suit and tie. Now everything you do with your hands is respected. My dad was a printer and bookbinder but my parents wanted me to be a civil engineer.

I was obsessed with trying to understand how objects function: my approach was to break them apart and figure it out. That triggered my interest in product design.

WHERE DO YOU FIND INSPIRATION?

My inspiration comes from the people around me, my family and friends. I like researching and reading about my culture, talking to others and asking questions. Why are things this way? I like to create design that makes you smile. There is a great power in happiness.

HOW DO YOU SEE BRITISH DOMESTIC INTERIORS EVOLVING?

We have become very intelligent consumers. It's not about having a fancy this or that; people want to experience things. In the future we will all want interiors that are a reflection of ourselves – that have stories. It's about more than just buying an object, it's narratives; creating a personal space that reflects who you are.

WHAT ADVICE WOULD YOU GIVE SOMEONE TO HELP THEM BRING OUT THEIR OWN TASTE AND PERSONALITY IN THEIR HOMES?

I love the cultures that are a part of me. Early on I missed out on my culture because I was afraid of being different but when you are at home with your family you can be as free as you can be.

We are at a good time in design. Cultural identity is very important. It's what gives you a voice and allows you to be free and create a beautiful object. More designers and architects use their culture in their work. What I'm creating now is in line with who I am. Embrace your culture.

'For me colour is about celebration and remembering a moment, and these colours remind me of a particular personal time. I put happiness into my work.'

Textile and Wallpaper Designer

PETER GOMEZ

Originally from Gibraltar, designer Peter Gomez
moved to London to study at the London College
of Printing. He currently heads the design studio at
renowned British brand Zoffany, known for fabrics
and wallpapers that combine historical references,
innovative techniques and contemporary design.

'My style is characterised by bravery: having a mixture of scale, colour and technique all put together, which heightens impact.'

HIDDEN WITHIN A 1970S BLOCK OF FLATS ON THE SHORES OF THE RIVER THAMES IN WEST LONDON IS THE VIBRANT HOME SHARED BY DESIGNER PETER GOMEZ, HIS PARTNER AND THEIR WELL-BEHAVED CAT.

The waterside development, which was originally a trans-shipment point for goods between the railway network and barges on the river, was created by the Greater London Council and now includes the Brentford Dock Marina and Brentford Dock Estate.

In contrast to the more typical towers of the 1970s, the block was designed by architect Sir Roger Walter in a low-rise style, and the development has blossomed into a tranquil neighbourhood surrounded by greenery, light and public spaces set within the last remnants of the area's industrial past.

Opening a glossy black front door (with cat flap) you step into Peter's small entrance hall, which is simply but precisely decorated. A staircase leads up to the main level giving the flat privacy and a dignified elegance.

'This is the first property we've owned and it's our first attempt to re-design it all,' says Peter. 'The result is a home that is very much a reflection of ourselves. My partner is not a designer so it's important I keep my eyes open to ideas that one would not normally consider. At home I try not to be the answer to everything. Living in a shared space is more of a learned behaviour for me. Whenever a decorating suggestion is made, I stop, breathe and listen to understand where it's coming from. Dialogue and compromise are very important.' Considering all the beautiful textiles, one suspects that Peter, who is used to leading a successful studio at one of the UK's top interior brands and is often tapped by the press for his views on trends and design, may get away with a lot.

Once the couple got the flat's layout just the way they wanted it, rather than fill it quickly, they decided to wait until they found the right furniture. 'We are buying things that we're investing in for our lives rather than buying something for a specific space,' confides Peter. 'Having previously lived in a rental it was a pleasure moving in with some things we already had and great fun waiting to spot a special piece in markets like Sunbury Antiques in Kempton or shops at favourite historic towns like Chichester in West Sussex.'

In his professional life Peter operates in a hectic environment surrounded by a creative orderly mess. The Zoffany studio is open-plan to encourage his team's designers to explore and share ideas for the brand. They have at least two years' worth of collections in development up on their inspiration walls.

His flat is more edited. There are visually stimulating bursts of pattern, yet the interior manages to feel serene and cocooning because the walls are painted in Zoffany's 'Perfect White' and the pattern is contained. Occasionally Peter works from home at the dining room table facing a large window. Here, chairs from a charity shop upholstered in a development fabric from Zoffany have been paired with a vintage-looking table from American high-street shop West Elm. 'The chairs were originally covered in a corduroy effect rubber which had to go. We like the fact that they are comfortable and stack beautifully,' says Peter.

In a corner by the window is a mannequin. 'My partner used to be a costumier for West End theatre and the dining table also doubles as his sewing table where he happily creates garments purely for his own pleasure.'

The sideboard, another lucky charity-shop find, displays a revolving collection of objects, from Russian dolls to impulsive holiday buys. 'Sometimes I replace them with better items and donate what was there back to a charity shop,' Peter says.

'I was very creative from an early age and did Fine Art at A-level. When I came to London I first worked in illustrative art and then moved on to wallpaper design, which triggered my love for architecture and interiors. Arriving in England I discovered there were so many different avenues, many more than where I grew up, and so much to explore,' he explains.

Now that he lives in London, Peter finds inspiration everywhere. 'I enjoy the art galleries (favourites include the Royal Academy, the Barbican and the Wallace Collection) and frequenting exhibitions. I travel with work and love learning about different cultures. It's also a privilege working with the amazing Zoffany archive with its array of design styles, patterns and textures from across the eras. I'm very lucky to collaborate with some of the best mills in the world: we combine their new technology and our vision to push boundaries and develop unique designs.'

In the living room, a Zoffany sofa, handmade in England, is covered in a crewel embroidery development fabric faithfully reproducing an Indian tree of life design. 'This is one of the early versions of "Kashida", created when we were developing a design for the "Frangipani collection. I know how much work went into this product and am very proud to have it at home,' says Peter.

The ottoman is upholstered in 'Abstract 1928' for Zoffany's 'Icons' collection. Inspired by a modernist block print this is the original colourway of the document that inspired it and cleverly shows every kind of misprint and imperfection in order to achieve the look of the original. The 1960s green leather chair is an auction find and the Lego cat perched on the smoke-coloured glass-topped vintage side table was 'a Christmas present to keep

me occupied over the holidays,' he adds. The cushions are covered in a selection of Zoffany fabrics created by Peter and his team. 'They are a moveable feast: as new fabrics are launched I add new ones and rotate them.'

The items that find their way into his home do so because of the time spent creating them. Peter likes being surrounded by things whose provenance he knows and can appreciate.

Opposite the ottoman, an upholstered green armchair is covered in 'Nootka', a fine jacquard inspired by a canopy of conifer leaves that captures the realism of foliage in a jewel-like malachite colour. The simple curtains are an old Zoffany design in velvet on linen in 'a great shade of red which I liked from the moment I first saw it. It was a bit of a battle with my partner,' Peter confides.

Casually propped artwork includes architectural images of Naples and framed watercolour experiments on how colours mix, plus a large textural piece of artwork on the chrome console table.

Peter's style is an eclectic, impulsive mix of things he loves. 'I gather them over time. They include pieces that I've worked on collaboratively with colleagues. With other objects I've liked the aesthetic or the memories they hold. I gravitate towards things that are individual and bring them home and allow them to layer the surfaces. I'm drawn to colour and bold design. In my professional life I like creating designs that are aesthetically pleasing and evoke emotion. My style is characterised by bravery: having a mixture of scale, colour and technique all put together, which heightens impact. At home he advises, 'if you see something and find it emotive in a good way, trust your instincts and go with that. Start with your favourite pieces.'

In the bedroom a favourite wallpaper – 'Richmond Park' – covers the wall behind the metal bed. The cubist design on stacked vintage leather suitcases, which double as bedside tables, is a colour board made up of plain fabrics from Zoffany. The overscaled wood and glass cabinet found on eBay by Peter's partner is a sturdy vintage-shop display case converted into a wardrobe. The colourful shirts are not Peter's, revealing a shared love for pattern in this relationship.

In addition to pattern, history and craftsmanship are important in Peter's design work. 'I am very lucky to have access to the Zoffany archive. It is a bespoke archive that has been built up over the years and is very much the look of the brand. It is very organic with textiles specifically bought for our needs and it evolves as the brand evolves. You can draw on the experience and learnings of previous designers, but then build on these to create something totally new,' explains Peter.

'Artistry and craftsmanship are at the core of what I do as a designer,' he adds. 'We create artwork and build up concepts in the studio and through our relationship with our manufacturers around the world. We nurture our relationships with our manufacturers to develop new techniques and they help us reinterpret our archive and make it relevant for today. We also embrace technology in both design and manufacture. It is important to challenge convention to innovate. I think the standout elements of British design have often been about non-conforming. Rules are constantly being broken because of new technology. For example, interior designers now adorn walls with digital panels that resemble fine art.'

However, Peter believes the elements of balance, proportion, colour and lighting will always be the foundation of all interiors, 'in the same way that in surface pattern design we will always need layout, pattern, repeat. 'The UK has a history of setting the bar in terms of what interior style is about – but

this unique history is constantly updated. We can confidently draw on our rich heritage of design from many eras to make them relevant for the current time. Over the years we have been good at appropriation – bringing back souvenirs from our trade routes and travels but making them our own. Paisley came from India; it is very much an Indian/Middle Eastern design motif brought over to the UK by the Victorians and then manufactured in Scotland for shawls. Something that was created elsewhere is absorbed and becomes a staple in design and interior design. It then becomes part of our design language. At Zoffany, graphic flame stitches and paisleys replace the gap filled by a floral pattern in another brand's collection. They introduce pattern and colour but in a more gender-neutral way.'

At home Peter has allowed his interior to develop organically with elements being layered over the course of time, and the confidence to let his own personality shine through.

Antiques Dealer and
Interior Decorator

JACK
LAVER
BRISTER

Jack Laver Brister is a young dealer/decorator who lives in the present with a great love and appreciation for the past. Having grown up in relaxed, unpretentious interiors, from an early age he was taken by his antiques dealer grandfather on buying trips to flea markets, auctions and fairs. Jack's style has developed from these experiences and the familiar surroundings that he describes as having a comfortable, well-loved feel, with a layered look.

Known as 'Tradchap' by his many Instagram followers, he deals in country-house furniture, soft furnishings and lighting. The decorating side of his business grew in response to customers admiring his personal style and knack for conjuring antiques-filled spaces that look like they have always been there.

His current shop is in south Somerset, in a colonial-style building with a tin roof overlooking open fields. It attracts a broad customer base from private clients through to members of the trade. His pieces are never over-restored, often in original condition, with the character of the patina gained through their age still apparent. He tends to source items he would have in his own house, including glazed cabinets, column lamps, whimsical dining chairs, oil portraits and decorative items found on his travels.

HOW DO YOU DEFINE YOUR STYLE?

My style is inspired by a traditional English country house evolved over generations. I love big feather-filled sofas, relaxed armchairs and loose covers. My look is made modern by injecting one or two twentieth-century pieces into it, usually with history or an interesting provenance.

WHAT SETS BRITISH DESIGN APART?

Tradition and quality, by which I mean good, well-made pieces of furniture that look like they are, or could have been, inherited. The same items, such as mahogany bookcases and chintz fabrics, have been in vogue for generations. You can mix and match different eras and styles for a layered look.

Colour and pattern have always been important, from the bold pastel colours against white plasterwork that characterise the interiors of Scottish neoclassical architect Robert Adam, to work by design legends of the twentieth century such as David Mlinaric, Nancy Lancaster and David Hicks.

ARE THERE ANY DESIGN RULES ANYMORE?

Good design doesn't need rules. You should go with what feels right, looking carefully at the context and feel of the space. Get a feel of a room by looking at original features and work around those rather than change the room. You can work with what you've got and then enhance. If there are no original features you bring your own features. A good fire surround makes a room – it doesn't have to be expensive, it can be made of wood. Or you can choose an impressive piece of furniture to create a focal point.

WHAT DO YOU MOST LIKE ABOUT YOUR SHOP?

I like the fact that it's a light airy white space, which is great for displaying furniture. I rearrange it once a month depending on what comes in and out. My shop is not a room set, it has a domestic sensibility. I try to give the sense of a grand living room, playing with scale, bringing in plants and colour.

WHAT MADE YOU WANT TO BECOME A DESIGNER?

I grew up in rooms with interesting textiles, wallpapers and family furniture that was not new but had come down through different generations. Family houses inspired me from an early age, as well as some that are open to the public – Lanhydrock in Cornwall, Calke Abbey in Derbyshire and Tyntesfield in north Somerset. My grandparents were both dealers and auctioneers so there's always been a family passion for objects. Design, however, is not such a family thing. My relations were very much dealers while I like creating beautiful spaces. The things I buy aren't always practical, but I like to think they are beautiful.

WHAT ARE THE KEY ELEMENTS OF A MODERN, PERSONAL AND STYLISH INTERIOR?

A space that is usable but beautiful and timeless. Being functional is what makes it modern. I always focus on making a traditional look liveable and purposeful.

WHERE DO YOU FIND INSPIRATION?

Inspiration is everywhere, but I find visiting country houses, period books such as the Country Life books and old issues of the magazine particularly inspiring. And of course, Instagram has revolutionised finding reference images.

HOW DO YOU SEE BRITISH DOMESTIC INTERIORS EVOLVING?

I see a move away from minimalism towards natural finishes and beautiful objects. There is a revolution against mass production, 'made in China' and the cheaply made. We are gravitating towards objects that are made to last. I'd certainly rather buy something that will last forever.

WHAT ADVICE WOULD YOU GIVE SOMEONE TO HELP THEM BRING OUT THEIR OWN TASTE AND PERSONALITY?

Employ me – but perhaps I am being biased.

Clients and people in general sometimes gravitate towards pieces that are safe and boring. In my role I draw out what they really like giving them the confidence to express who they are. Once I understand their taste I can design bespoke interiors around them and their preferences that will last into the future.

Designer

MELINA BLAXLAND -HORNE

Born in Greece, British designer Melina Blaxland-Horne is known for creating striking handmade lampshades and a growing collection of colourful lamps and cushions. As a child, Melina was drawn to fabrics, patterns and colour. Both her mother, who carefully restored the family home, as well as her great-grandmother, a successful milliner, became an important inspiration.

Her company – 'Melodi Horne' – supplies bespoke lampshades to in-the-know interior designers who seek unique products that are handmade in England and appreciate Melina's attention to detail.

Created with fabrics sourced from around the world, including the UK, Melina's designs are seldom neutral or simply functional. They are statement pieces with the power to create a mood and a special ambience.

WHAT SETS BRITISH DESIGN APART?

British design is bold, expressive, outrageous, purposeful, innovative, beautiful, daring and at times provocative but it never takes itself too seriously! It combines a certain sense of fun and humour – just like the British – without becoming ridiculous.

ARE HISTORY AND CRAFTSMANSHIP IMPORTANT IN YOUR DESIGN WORK?

History and craftsmanship are essential to my work. They are both part of what inspires me.

As a new traditionalist, who combines old skills to create my contemporary work, I often look to historical trends and styles then reinvent them with a twist that's relevant to today's world, taking care not to create something too kitsch. My lampshades, for example, have traditional construction and yet are reimagined in a riot of colourful linen linings. Our handcrafted lampstands can even be painted to match the linings to create a colour block effect.

Out of love for my work, I try to do as much as I can myself, but also commission a small group of skilled artisans who help develop and manufacture our products. At Melodi Horne we support a cottage industry of craftspeople and luckily come across like-minded individuals who absolutely love their trade. We collaborate with small, family-run businesses such as our carpenters, framers and skilled colleagues some who work from a shed in their garden and who lovingly remain true to their craft.

I have great respect for our clients and this is reflected in the quality and craftsmanship of our work.

HOW ABOUT TECHNOLOGY?

We live in a world dominated by technology, which is a great asset as long as we don't forget our skills and our history.

British designers are very clever and forward-thinking when it comes to bringing technology and craftsmanship together. All one needs to do is to look at the magnificent Victorian Tower Bridge, exceptional for its historically-inspired style, innovative nineteenth-century steel and concrete construction and the fact that it is still completely functional today.

Lighting, my field, is always evolving and as a designer I feel that it is very important to keep up to date with the trends, while using the latest technology to improve our products.

Connectivity, for example, is a trend in lighting technology: digitally controlling one's lighting or operating it via remote control, or through voice command. The introduction of LED lights has also become a popular innovation which is taking over traditional lighting. We have changed all our wall lights to LED which means the lamps don't heat up and are dimmable. LED also saves on energy, making our beautiful products more eco-friendly.

A manufacturer like me sees technology as a tool for improving their product and making it unique for a period of time, until everyone else catches up!

ARE THERE ANY DESIGN RULES ANYMORE? HOW DO YOU BREAK THEM?

There are always design rules but like most things, rules are made to be broken by introducing new concepts and ideas!

This question is extremely relevant to my studio because we regularly break rules.

When I started my company I was once advised by a very well-known and accomplished designer that one cannot use anything other than cream/white silk linings in lampshade-making in order to maximise the light. He was adamant about it because at the time this was the lampshade norm, however, I begged to differ.

At my studio we challenged the traditional approach to lampshade making by not only introducing linen linings but also by launching the use of over 50 different lining colours, something that to my knowledge is not done elsewhere.

Our concept was that a lampshade isn't just a functional lighting object, it is an integral part of one's soft furnishings (just like cushions on a sofa, or curtains). A shade is a statement piece and each coloured lining creates a different mood in a room.

A soft pink lining brings tranquility and calm, navy blue will create a cool boudoir, almost smoky look and an orange lining will bathe one's room in a warm sunset. The linen itself has so much texture and so many holes that it almost becomes translucent, forcing the light to travel to the outer fabric creating the most wonderful effect.

We have continued to challenge design rules of lighting by creating our 'Bon-Bon' wall lights, with frames manufactured in a range of finishes, such as timber, bronze, oxidised and powder-coated steel in any colour the client wishes. One can choose card, fabric, wallpaper, leather or any other material as a central panel and change the interior panel as often as one wants.

Again, to my knowledge this is something unique. Our concept here is to offer immediate choice, change and personalisation by allowing our clients to add their own creative stamp.

WHAT IS YOUR FAVOURITE CORNER OF YOUR STUDIO AND WHY?

My linen colour palette on the wall across from where I sit because it inspires me and never fails to cheer me up.

WHAT MADE YOU WANT TO BECOME A DESIGNER?

Without a doubt my childhood and early surroundings. I grew up in an 1827 neoclassical house with intricately-corniced high ceilings, richly painted walls in deep colours (olives, browns and terracotta mixed with lighter colours) and marquetry herringbone floorboards.

My mother used her tremendous creativity, restoring and decorating the house in the most exquisite way. She had no fear of clashing colour, mixing a yellow with a coral hue, for example. This fearlessness is something that I have brought to my work and comes very naturally. I remember witnessing the process as a little girl, and I learned that colours all work together.

My parents were antique collector hobbyists. I was educated in beautiful things and knew well-known porcelain makers like Limoges, Sèvres and Jacob Petit from the early age of four. I remember studying each piece with wonderment and fascination because of its

shape, colour and details. I caught the design bug at a very young age and knew from then on that I wanted to be making beautiful things – I wanted to be creating lights especially. Their brightness was the first thing that fascinated me. As an adult I appreciate the mood a light creates. According to my parents, my first word was light – '*lamba*' in Greek. Perhaps it was a little clue into my future.

WHERE DO YOU FIND INSPIRATION?

It starts from within – from emotions, such as love and passion. I see an object that I like and my mind translates it into so many other possibilities. For example, I see an object like a door knob or cornice and may turn it into an inspiration for a lamp stand. I sketch a lot and then I tap into those things that caught my eye and develop them into products.

I am often inspired by travel, old textiles, Georgian architecture, John Nash, the 1970s, ancient Egypt, Art Deco, antiques, descriptive literature, nature, visits to historical sites and museums.

WHAT ADVICE WOULD YOU GIVE SOMEONE TO HELP THEM BRING OUT THEIR OWN TASTE AND PERSONALITY?

Know yourself and be confident in what you have to offer. Be proud to share it with the rest of the world because you are unique.

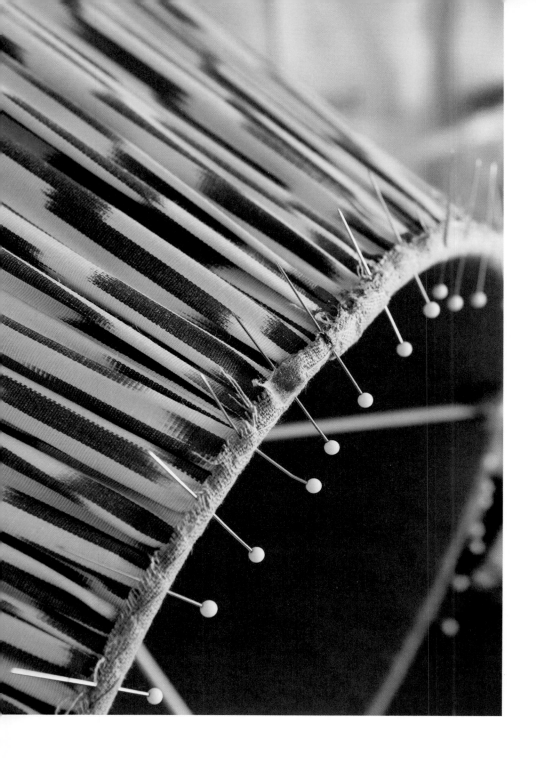

Colour Specialist and Marketing Director

RUTH MOTTERSHEAD

Ruth Mottershead joined her family's Little Greene company (which also owns the Paint & Paper Library brand) eight years ago. Originally trained as a landscape architect she previously worked on urban design and National Trust gardens before later completing a master's degree in digital marketing.

Ruth is responsible for the British group's paint colours and trend direction as well as overseeing the wallpaper ranges' development from archive material to final design. Her remit also extends to creative direction for the advertising campaigns, marketing and design. Ruth regularly hosts inspiring colour workshops in the UK and internationally.

Her modern house in the countryside near the village of Hale surrounded by horses and endless rural views offers a much-needed escape. Ruth commutes to the company's nearby headquarters in Manchester where the collections are created, and regularly visits the company's showrooms across Europe.

HOW DO YOU DEFINE YOUR STYLE?

Working with colour and pattern every day has a real influence on me and naturally both elements feature throughout my home. The way I have designed my interior reflects my character. I enjoy bold colours (like the 'Kigali' blue and 'Porcelain V' paints from Paint & Paper Library in my bedroom) and busy patterns just as much as I love natural materials and restful tones (like the 'Abbey Garden' wallpaper in 'Vert' that I used in the guest bedroom). For me, the concept of a space depends on the room and how it will be used, but in my own house I chose a mix of subtle and strong shades as well as an abundance of texture and pattern.

My home is a place to begin and to end my day and, of course, to enjoy all of those moments in between – a place to relax or entertain in an environment that has a mixture of all sorts of things that mean something to me. I have slowly accumulated items from places I have been, like the artwork above my teal sofa picked up at a student art fair, and the original William Morris print bought at auction above my bed, family pieces that have special memories and, of course, the collections we have spent hours working on at Little Greene all make up my style – a little mix of everything!

WHAT SETS BRITISH DESIGN APART?

Design forms a key part of British history and the manufacturing industry we still have here in Britain today really represents our heritage of 'making'. My husband and I are both from manufacturing families and we are both very proud of that. The quality of British products is internationally recognised and certainly the British manufacturing and design industries not only strive to make products that are beautifully designed but also to create products that last. The highly skilled workforce that are making things in this country put their love, attention and time into their work and I think this passion is reflected in British products.

ARE THERE ANY DESIGN RULES?

I don't believe there are any design rules anymore – we are living in a world where we should feel free to show our personality through the style of our interiors.

However, in the world of paint and wallpaper, I come across many people who are afraid to use colour in their home. The difficulty of choosing and combining colour is something that my colleagues and I are asked to help with every day.

I have a few personal principles that I like to share to create a professional interior:

- Paint the ceiling the same colour as your walls (unless, of course, you want to create a statement ceiling). Painting them the same colour means the eye is not naturally drawn to a white ceiling – other aspects of a room become more important.

- Don't spend too much time thinking about how to make a room look more spacious; instead harness the size of a room and focus on making it more cosy and comfortable.

White will not a make a room look bigger. Darker colours make a room more intimate. In my snug next to the kitchen I've gone for a dark colour – 'Lamp Black' – and a Little Greene wallpaper called 'Carlton House Terrace'.

- Use colour in proportion. When choosing colour always look at tones in the proportions you will be using them in your room. If you are putting together a scheme with colour samples and planning on painting a skirting board in a darker tone and a wall in a neutral, compare a very small amount of the darker tone against a much larger amount of your intended wall colour – this will give you a real idea of how the colours will work together.

- If you are going to use white then don't use brilliant white; for me it can be very blue and quite harsh on the eye. Pick an off-white or a white with a base pigment that also features in another colour within your chosen scheme.

WHAT DO YOU MOST LIKE ABOUT YOUR HOUSE?

Our house is situated on the site of an old farmhouse and the wildlife and farm animals outside make it a very relaxing place to be.

I enjoy being in the living room, mainly because of the view out of the window. An afternoon can easily slip away while sitting on the velvet sofa reading a book or enjoying the scenery even on a rainy day. The living room walls are painted in Little Greene's 'Livid', a bold, yet muted green which almost brings the outside in. We have paired this colour with the soft 'China Clay Deep' on the upper wall and ceiling for a really harmonious, tranquil interior. To me, green and pink are a warm and cosy combination. To make our sofa extra comfortable I like having a throw and

oversized linen cushions and I have a little table by it that I can move around easily.

WHAT IS YOUR FAVOURITE CORNER?

My favourite corner is probably my laundry room because we have really been adventurous and carefree with our colour and pattern choices! It is a reflection of busy, everyday life and, if truth be told, it is usually a little disorganised. My husband chose the wallpaper – a fabulous jungle design he printed at his factory and I paired it with Little Greene's 'Trumpet' for a really lively, engaging and playful space. It is also where our puppy sleeps and to come down and see her every morning is always a real treat.

WHAT MADE YOU WANT TO WORK IN THE DESIGN INDUSTRY?

I have always had a love for design and art and have been surrounded by creativity all of my life. My father David Mottershead, who founded Little Greene, is the same and was always very encouraging of me pursuing design as a career. We have spent many days together visiting art galleries, sculpture parks and travelling. I undertook a design degree in landscape architecture through which I gained a professional qualification designing urban spaces, parks and heritage sites.

After working in London as a landscape architect, I moved to join the family business, which was a natural transition from designing exterior spaces to interior design. When you study spatial design you apply similar parameters to any space whether exterior or interior. There are relevant issues to consider such as how you use the space, how it works and how you move around it. Its function and character are important, so whether it's historical or contemporary is something that needs to be taken into account whether you are designing a garden or a room. My experience working on historical sites and gardens helped my approach when we design wallpaper inspired by archival material.

WHAT ARE THE KEY ELEMENTS OF A MODERN, PERSONAL AND STYLISH INTERIOR?

For me, it is important first and foremost to ensure you are surrounded by the things you love, be it art or photographs, special family pieces or items that evoke memories.

When it comes to furniture, I suggest trying to reflect the character of the house. Mine is very modern so I respect that aspect of the architecture and have gone for a clean look. You can also incorporate antiques if you want but remember the reality of your specific interior. Because our views are beautiful we wanted to keep things edited so not to distract from the outside.

If you're moving into your first house like us, it is important that pieces can be moved around and allow you to make changes as your life evolves. Our house has been put together as a cohesive scheme where most items have similar clean lines in materials like metal and wood; the furniture is upholstered in textured fabrics. The pieces are integral but moveable from room to room. This consistency creates a calm and flexible environment.

To style a contemporary interior, don't be afraid to use colour. I personally love strongly contrasting schemes with two bold opposing colours, as I've used in my bedroom.

WHERE DO YOU FIND INSPIRATION?

I find inspiration from many different sources. Working in a manufacturing environment means I am lucky to be surrounded by creative processes and creative people on a daily basis. Travel is important; I spend quite a lot of time in different countries – Germany, France where we have showrooms or Russia and Holland to visit stockists – experiencing other cultures and meeting people which often pushes me to think in new ways. Fashion is a big influence – watching the progression of trends, particularly the way colour and pattern are used in combination and understanding how these elements change each season. There is a clear link between fashion and interiors and often the colours of the catwalk relate to on-trend colours in the home.

History is a very important part of our design process. We collaborate with organisations such as the National Trust to create new collections. The 'Green' capsule collection of colours for Little Greene was inspired by some of England's oldest buildings. 'Windmill Lane', a soft muted green, came about from research at the main stair at Osterley Park, and research at Hill Top, Beatrix Potter's former farm in the Lake District, led us to develop 'Sage and Onions'. This bright green colour is inspired by Jemima Puddle-Duck and the original garden gate at the property. Each of the personalities and locations involved in the design and making of a collection are central to creating our products. When designing a new collection, we always start with archive pieces and develop new designs from there.

HOW DO YOU SEE BRITISH DOMESTIC INTERIORS EVOLVING?

British domestic interiors are evolving thanks to developments in digital technology. There are now these big printers that use special inks to print wallpapers, and also social media, which provides a platform through which consumers can share and view interior inspiration. The ability to see what other people are doing in their homes, to be able to follow influencers and understand what brands are doing, what's on trend and view 'how to' videos has increased consumer confidence to make choices by themselves and be their own interior designer.

Colour palettes constantly shift in different directions and style adapts and evolves depending on the different spaces we inhabit. Pattern comes in and out of fashion and the British interiors industry is thriving – there are so many designers and brands doing a tremendous job, such as Cole & Son and Morris & Co, which encompass the best of British and build on an archive of fantastic product history. There is a deep respect for designers and artists of the past, such as sculptors Henry Moore and Barbara Hepworth, which is engrained within our heritage and I believe designers will always look to Britain's past as a source of inspiration. William Morris and the Arts and Crafts movement had a huge influence on the interior industry and this is still felt in domestic interiors today. Quality is important and expected within the industry.

There will be more colour, more design and boundaries are being, and will continue to be, pushed from all angles regarding the making, the design and the changing technology. Companies will continue to strive to create products in the UK – it's an exciting time ahead for our industry.

'Design forms a key part of British history and the manufacturing industry we still have here in Britain today really represents our heritage of "making".'

Artist and Designer

MINNIE KEMP

The self-described 'kick-ass' colourist is an interior designer at her family's business, Firmdale Hotels. Minnie, known for her love of pattern, contributes her wonderful visual sense to the design team's projects. Not afraid to step away from the norm, Minnie likes interiors that are layered, fun, relaxed and English.

'London is a cultural melting pot of wonderfulness, with Brits who have heritages from all over the world. British design is fearless – for a tiny island we pack a punch.'

IN LEAFY SOUTH KENSINGTON, AROUND THE CORNER FROM LONDON'S MUSEUM QUARTER, SITS FIRMDALE HOTELS' DESIGN OFFICE.

The elegant stucco-fronted nineteenth-century townhouse on a residential terrace hides a riot of colour, pattern, fabrics and art. These are the hallmark ingredients of the joyful aesthetic championed by founder Kit Kemp for her eight London and two New York hotels.

Daughter Minnie Kemp is a tornado of energy. She welcomes us and guides us up and up the stairs – its walls are used as art storage for a gallery's worth of historic sepia-coloured and black and white engravings in cheery hand-painted frames which are on their way to or from the boutique hotel company's constantly renewed rooms.

Minnie's tiny private lair, a light-filled single room, is an Aladdin's cave of lamps, cushions, fabric swatch books, and the quirkiest travel souvenirs – assuming Aladdin had very eclectic taste and owned a well-used sewing machine.

A high window frames the V&A's dome and the designer's large desk is placed facing one of the world's leading museums of art and design.

'I like being opposite the V&A – it's a treasure trove of inspiration on my doorstep. Who could ask for more?' she enthuses. 'I remember when we were designing and building the Ham Yard Hotel, I was also writing my graphic design dissertation and spending a lot of time in the V&A's National Art Library. On one visit I noticed a tiny small-scale spiral orange press thingy at the café downstairs – needless to say instead of doing any actual essay work I spent the next hour drawing a gigantic orange spiral sculpture that we now have in the Dive Bar at the hotel.'

With this sort of creative energy, it's no surprise that Minnie has become a designer.

'It does sort of run in the family!' laughs Minnie. 'My mother is a living legend and completely design-obsessed. She used to take us on building sites hanging off one hip.' Minnie's sister, Willow Kemp, is a trained architect who created the drawings for ceramics that Kit Kemp designed for Wedgwood, and her father, Tim, is a perfectionist with an amazing eye, who finds the properties that the hotel group develops. Tim is known for being very charming and gets what he wants – a description, one soon discovers, could also apply to Minnie. 'My parents have been buying plots and building boutique hotels since before I was born. They are workaholics and I'm so proud and inspired by them,' she says. 'When I was small, we lived next to the design studio. After school I could usually be found scribbling on the walls of the project office, where all the buildings' technical details and electrics are planned.'

Her greatest love is travelling to source products and discover new textiles, furniture and artists. 'One of the big pulls of being an artist/designer is the idea that you can do your work anywhere and at any time. You aren't tied to one place: so long as you have your laptop, sketchbook and pens you are free to roam, as well as shop and haul back amazing finds,' Minnie says.

On mood boards to the left of her door are all sorts of postcards, tassels and textiles – usually handmade (although some mass trinkets that catch her sharp eye, and treasures with a story to inspire future projects, do make the edit). 'I'm attracted to things that I can use in my own work, which help develop colour, pattern and mood. I seem always to bring back hand-embroidered clothes. A detail or stitch can spark a scheme for a bedroom suite. There are no rules. I'm constantly moving forward and not getting stuck,' she confides. 'You never know where or what might trigger an idea. You could be on the tube opposite a man reading poems of Lord Byron, which could spark a green, purple and goldish flora design (a true story).' Or it could be chatting with her dear friend Ruby Kean who looks after Firmdale's New York properties. They are best friends in a creative way, which means she's not afraid to be very honest. 'Bouncing ideas around with friends makes you feel anything is possible – collaboration is a real adventure. I love it!'

Next on Minnie's inspiration-hunting schedule is a big trip to the remote Trobriand Islands, an archipelago in Papua New Guinea. 'I'm really interested in photographing and learning about the intricately-carved yam houses, and look forward to trying some ebony carving. This dense black hardwood is abundant there.'

In her work Minnie is fascinated by colours – from vibrant and punchy to more dusky tones. 'I enjoy seeing how different shades pop in an interior and create a completely new feeling. Or discovering that in-between hue, resulting when colours kiss. When you get the right balance the whole essence of the room feels right – that makes me really happy.' Her colour palette is always evolving. 'There is a real unbridled freedom in being able to design a room or a textile combining the shade of yellow in the egg you had for breakfast with your sky-blue nail polish to create something bespoke.'

She often works in historic buildings and likes to respond directly to their environment while considering the setting. This means the style can vary according to each project, even if Minnie inevitably adds her stamp. She may have the idea for the perfect fabric in her head but can't find it so she will source wool felt and stitch it herself to achieve the perfect look.

When it comes to furniture, the designer tends to repurpose: she transformed trunks from a vintage market into a mini bar for the Dorset Square Hotel, and an old stork weathervane now serves as a floor lamp at the Knightsbridge Hotel (around the corner from Minnie's office

and which she showed us on our visit to Firmdale).

'We are also inspired by history,' says Minnie. 'Our Haymarket Hotel's exterior was designed by John Nash, the architect who also designed Buckingham Palace. Most of the generously-sized rooms have very tall ceilings and a dado rail, which look better with a stripe or a mixture of scales of pattern . Below the dado rail I use a smaller pattern and then allow a larger scale design above giving it space to breathe and adding dramatic interest. Vertical stripes enhance the height making a room look a lot bigger and grander. Just like in fashion you want to enhance the positives. It's fun to work with a building like that and you don't have to do much because the decorative architecture speaks for itself. Our more contemporary loft-style buildings like the Soho Hotel look much better with slick wall-to-wall linen and funky lights.

'When I see bad interior design it makes me feel dizzy and sick.' In Minnie's mind bad is either too busy or without focus. To be avoided are dark heavy interiors where you can't relax and feel weighed down, as opposed to light, fresh, inclusive and caring. 'I actually have to leave the room,' she says. 'Sometimes it's the folk with the biggest budget that seem to desecrate spaces!' Her top decorating tip is to surround yourself with furniture, art and textiles that make you happy and that mean something to you. 'When you try to please others it's never going to work.

'And think BIG!' she adds. 'Cutesy bits are… well, cute, and certainly have a place, but it's so refreshing to edit and leave space in an interior.' For Minnie, organic shapes and natural wood (including old elm and petrified wood) are queen, and don't forget house plants, 'especially in cities where we all crave greenery'. Minnie recommends visiting flea markets like Kempton (Sunbury Antiques Market), or even abroad – she ventures to

Long Island and upstate New York, as well as Houston in Texas. Whatever you do, 'don't freak out and buy everything new,' urges Minnie. 'A home is built up over time. Remember that an exciting interior is like a tapestry with many layers.

'London is a cultural melting pot of wonderfulness, with Brits who have heritages from all over the world – I love seeing this shine through the creative fields. British design is fearless – for a tiny island we pack a punch. I get really inspired by women like Grace Wales Bonner, founder of London-based menswear label Wales Bonner, whom I've known since I was a child. A polymath, daughter of a Jamaican father and English mother, she can spend no money and make the most beautiful things. Her collection explores representations of black male identity through exceptional craftsmanship and embellishments. I also love companies such as The New Craftsmen, which champion craft and its makers.'

With an eye to what's next for her and the broader design scene, 'Britain is at the forefront of sustainable design, which is the future. We can all be inspired by Petra Palumbo, the Scottish Highlands-based company known for lovely sustainable home accessories. I like Petra's work because her creations are colourful and fun and beautiful but happen to have an environmental conscience. There's a gap in the market and we need to expose people to being more sustainable in the interiors world,' believes Minnie. 'I'm also looking forward to the current masculine 1950s style being locked away in a cupboard, never to return. I hope we are moving more towards sustainable living with ethically-sourced textiles and more sumptuous recycled furniture that doesn't look like grandma's breakfast. I want to see renewable energy being made sexy and allotments on roofs. Just because it's ethical it doesn't mean it has to be boring,' continues Minnie. 'There are loads of amazing natural dyes: I absolutely love Dyeworks started by Polly Lyster. She is amazing with colour and her sample bag of hand-dyed fabric swatches has helped me a lot.'

And how would Minnie advise others regarding their own decorating projects? 'Start a scrapbook and put cuttings of everything you like in there. After time you will start to see a trend and you can build up an idea of suppliers you like and designers that inspire you and colours that turn you on. The best blog I know out there is KitKemp.com – it has thousands of top interior design tips you can all try at home.'

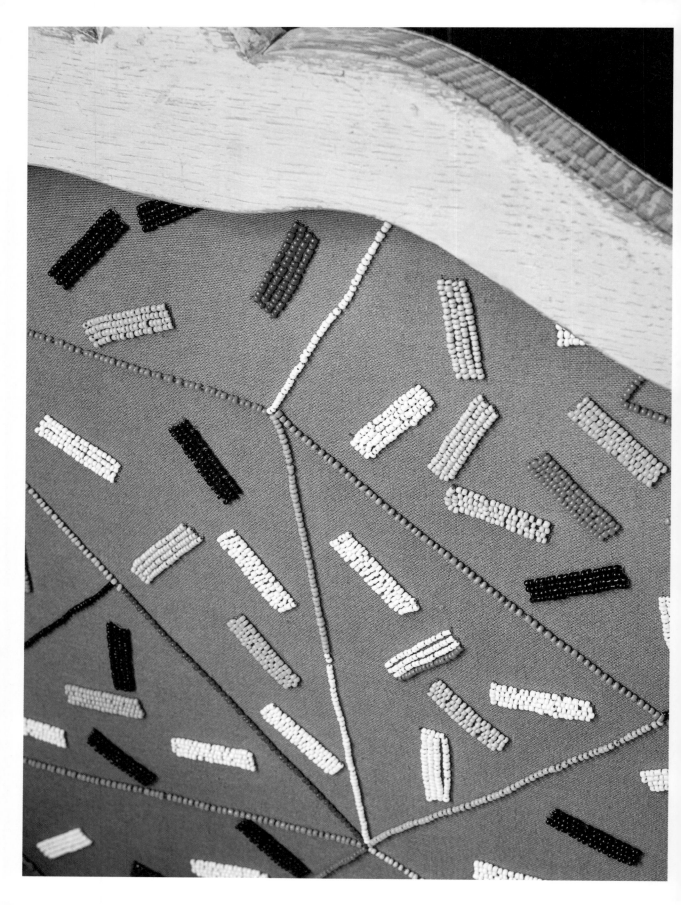

Design Director

CHARLIE
BOWLES

Oxford-born designer Charlie Bowles is a director at his family's Original BTC lighting manufacturing company.

Working from offices in London, Charlie is immersed in all areas of the business, from design and manufacturing to sales, marketing and the ongoing expansion of the brand internationally, which includes overseeing showrooms in London, Paris and New York.

Having started his professional career assembling the brand's iconic 'Hector' collection and working on the company's stand at Maison & Objet (the influential Paris design fair) as a teenager, Charlie progressed to designing the Original BTC website and brochures while studying Product Design at Leeds University. Charlie's first lamp design was the 'London' in 2009, the same year he joined the company full time. An instant classic, the mid-century style light remains one of Original BTC's best-loved designs.

He currently lives in an 1880s painted brick townhouse in Barnes, south-west London.

HOW DO YOU DEFINE YOUR STYLE?

My style is eclectic. I'm not going for a specific look at home – I just slowly add things that my wife Anna and I like as we go along. In our house I wanted to create a relaxing interior.

With my choice of lighting I focused on the reflection of warm light throughout our home. In the living room, for example, lamps made of brushed brass and white bone china add warmth when they are flicked on. The furnishings include a large gold convex mirror, textured fabrics and honey-coloured floors to add to this effect, creating an edited space that feels modern and welcoming.

WHAT SETS BRITISH DESIGN APART?

Personality and attention to detail.

At home, personality for me is having pieces that mean something to you. We have lights from Original BTC that I have been involved in designing and creating, as well as mirrors from my wife Anna's family company English Georgian, made bespoke with a grey inset. The clock on the mantlepiece belonged to my great, great uncle who was in the Royal Air Force. The centre is made from an airplane propeller and next to it artillery shells from WWI have been turned into brass pots and placed at either end of the mantle. Throughout the house there are things that have meaning, including paintings by my mother, artist Julia Bowles. Family history is subtly woven into our space.

Detail includes lighting, of course, and carefully selected accessories. In the living room a 'Chester' floor lamp creates a reading corner by the window and the navy velvet sofas get a jolt of bold graphic pattern from cushions designed by our Nottingham-based designer-friend Tori Murphy. A pair of 'Oxford' table lights on the side tables have subtle visual appeal with their twin bone-china shades. The comfortable wingchair by the fireplace is covered in a grey velvet and our 'Hatton 3' floor light with a faceted bone-china shade casts a subtle flattering light. Overhead, the 'Pembridge 3' pendant light has overlapping tiers of bone china, which gently diffuse light to enhance the atmospheric glow. There are often toys like the Steiff lion scattered about, as is the reality of living with kids. The patterned rug in yellow and grey brings colour into the room and a sense of fun.

ARE HISTORY AND CRAFTSMANSHIP IMPORTANT IN YOUR DESIGN WORK? HOW ABOUT TECHNOLOGY?

Craftsmanship is extremely important to me. At our company we have five different factories, each of which specialises in specific areas of manufacture. For example, our bone china comes from Stoke-on-Trent where we produce shades and pieces for our lights. All metal components are manufactured in Birmingham and we have a factory near Redditch where we hand-blow our glass.

It is these skills and craftsmanship that makes our products what they are and it is crucial we maintain them to ensure our products' uniqueness and quality.

Technology is always important as it can allow new processes and techniques to be introduced to enhance centuries'-old skills. It also enables designs that may not have been possible in the past to exist now.

ARE THERE ANY DESIGN RULES ANYMORE?

To be honest I have never taken any notice of any design rules – design is design; you can mostly do what you like! Integrity, however, is very important. BTC stands for British Timeless Classics. I like creating things with longevity that will stand the test of time. This means designing objects that people want now and will also want in 20 years' time.

WHAT DO YOU MOST LIKE ABOUT YOUR HOME?

I love how welcoming and happy our house is. It is a great space for entertaining. At Christmas we have eight to ten people over. Although not a big house you can open the double doors and extend the living room space into the kitchen.

The kitchen has very clean lines. I like to cook and when we entertain we dim the lights and create a cosy atmosphere enhanced by the light emanating from the 'Fin' horizontal pendant. The wood furniture by Dare Studio softens the space while keeping it contemporary.

WHAT IS YOUR FAVOURITE ROOM AND WHY?

My favourite room is the living room. I love the shuttered windows and the lit fire in winter. We spend a lot of time sitting there in the evenings. I also love my bedroom where we get the evening sun from our window.

WHAT MADE YOU WANT TO BECOME A DESIGNER?

I have always had an interest and passion for great design and coming from a family with roots in the design world just encouraged these. I remember going to factories with my dad Peter when I was young. He also always brought new products home and asked my sisters and me what we thought – whether we liked a lamp or the material – and we gave general feedback.

My mum is an artist and very creative. Growing up, our house was well considered and my mum would always be asking about colour and bouncing ideas off her children. She got us involved with helping her work out design solutions. She is also into photography and developed her photos at home which helped inform my visual sense.

WHERE DO YOU FIND INSPIRATION?

Inspiration can come from anywhere. Where design goes depends entirely on where my imagination takes me. At home inspiration comes from interiors that I've seen. I'm around different interiors all the time and regularly see things that I like.

In terms of design process in my professional life, we sometimes bring things out of the company archive; these are products that we think we can update and are relevant to now. Or I start out with drawing in my sketchbook, maybe based on something I saw in an old building, and then I play in my mind. We are also regularly listening to feedback from our customers, plus I'm travelling constantly seeing inspiring details on my trips.

FINE CELL WORK

Fine Cell Work (FCW) is a charity and social enterprise that enables prisoners and ex-prisoners to build fulfilling lives by making a living from their high-quality, skilled creative needlework. The charity's accomplished volunteers go into prisons fortnightly and run classes to teach new, and support existing, prison stitchers in the programme.

Operating from both the Fine Works Hub workshop in a Battersea brick mews building in south London, and in prisons across Britain, the charity supplies exquisite needlepoint and embroidery to some of the country's top interior designers and artists.

FCW'S AIM IS TO ALLOW PRISONERS TO FINISH THEIR SENTENCES WITH SKILLS, MONEY EARNED AND SAVED, AND THE SELF-BELIEF NOT TO RE-OFFEND. THE WORK OF THESE TALENTED MEN AND WOMEN, UNDERTAKEN IN THE LONG HOURS SPENT IN THEIR CELLS, FOSTERS HOPE, DISCIPLINE AND SELF-ESTEEM. ON RELEASE, THE CHARITY GUIDES THE EX-PRISONERS TOWARDS FURTHER TRAINING IN CRAFT AND OFFERS OTHER SUPPORT AND MENTORING TO HELP THEM WITH THEIR NEXT STEP IN LIFE.

Further employment and training also take place at the Fine Works Hub, where the charity runs the 'Open the Gate' post-prison programme, which provides work experience, formal training and employment to ex-prisoners, known as apprentices.

The Battersea studio is light, bright and always buzzing in a hive of activity – completed work coming in from prisons, apprentices finishing pieces to perfection, and staff coming and going. 'We have got a wonderfully wide range of threads and fabrics at the studio so it's a great place for interior designers to work out colour schemes by combining the many available options,' says the Workshop and Training Manager Wendy Cramer, who encourages creatives to pop in and engage with all that is possible to create in partnership with FCW.

The atmosphere is relaxed and the outside courtyard at the Fine Works Hub is popular in the summer when apprentices and staff go out to enjoy the sunshine and unwind. The team has planted herbs and the picnic tables are elbow-room-busy at lunch time. 'It's a great communal space and excellent place to catch up with apprentices and staff,' says Wendy.

FCW has a main collection of products, which it sells via its own website; it also creates skilfully-made bespoke pieces. FCW's work attracts some of the top names in design and art – with whom it collaborates on projects, including hotel owner Kit Kemp, fashion designer Stella McCartney (who commissioned a quilt that took two years to produce), interior designer Nicky Haslam and Chinese artist Ai Weiwei.

The range of collaborations and output has allowed FCW to forge strong links with top British producers. Textiles, for example, are often supplied by heritage companies that have been around for years – all of FCW's wools are spun in the UK and it sources linens from Scotland and Ireland.

Inspiration for the in-house design team employed by the charity comes from galleries, designer shows, antique markets, the natural world and antique textiles, plus their immediate community and camaraderie with designer-clients.

Hand-stitching is at the heart of FCW's style, and its products look sophisticated rather than homespun. Ultimately the prisoners make things that people want to buy and design products that appeal to the current market, with an edge. The result feels very special and well made, which is not surprising given that a cushion, for example, may require on average 100 hours of skilled work.

'Our style is defined by the exceptional craftsmanship of our products, unique designs and their unusual provenance,' says Executive Director Victoria Gillies. 'The cushions tell a story, and depending on which one you choose can provide the perfect pop of colour to a room. We have worked with a range of well-known creatives to develop collections that are beautifully conceived, and the stitch element can bring another dimension to the design. Making our cushions is a wonderful collaboration between the designer and the stitcher,' says Victoria.

'Many of our designs reference historical textiles, incorporating elements from these, such as "Pomegranate" inspired by an Ottoman motif. Most recently the "Bayeux Tapestry", which depicts the events leading to the Norman conquest of England, inspired a collaboration with an artist, and Jacobean crewel work was used in a cushion design. When colouring our designs, we often look to artists' work: Matisse, Modigliani and the German Bauhaus movement have all served as inspiration for recent designs,' reveals Victoria.

Craftsmanship is extremely important to the charity's products. As one of the stitchers points out, 'perfection isn't usually expected in prison,' but FCW's products often change people's view of what can be achieved there and its stitchers are proud of what they have created.

Beyond the hand-produced items, 'technology is important as we design on computer and produce all of our needlepoint charts with a specific charting programme,' explains Victoria, 'though we will always stitch a small sample before progressing with any project. It's amazing how different colours can look when they are stitched. Computer-aided design can never show the true effect of the stitching realistically.

'When we design we always take into account the stitcher as well as the end product. If the item is too boring, repetitive or complex for an individual then we will run into problems when we go into production. The FCW production team selects the specific person and skill level to ensure the best result. It is important to remember that our workforce includes people who have led complicated lives. Some people like repetition and a more formulaic approach; others are the opposite and want to sit there and hold their concentration as they are challenged by more intricate work. We understand our workforce, which allows us to take on projects that we

know will feed into a range of skill levels and help us match the therapeutic need/charitable purpose as well as meeting the customer's brief,' says Victoria.

'In terms of British design, it's the innovation and personality that sets us apart from others,' Victoria tells us. FCW breaks design rules and expectations with a production process that is unique. It works in several different prisons and some items can go in and out of cells three times until they are completed. One of FCW's biggest challenges is the production time, which is lengthy; its own collection has to be forward-thinking and at the forefront of creativity because its pieces can take years to hit the market. In addition, the rules and regulations it has to comply with means it faces logistical challenges. There are restrictions on the size of the items allowed into a prison, for example. Materials for a design arrive at the FCW workshop first, then they are put together in a kit with everything needed to assemble a design, including fabric, thread and relevant tools. The kit then goes to the stitchers, who work in their cells. After that a volunteer brings the piece back to the Hub. It gets checked by the volunteer stitchers and the production team then goes back into prison for adjustments and to complete the finished product.

'We're not just a production house, our products are made by people living in the bleakest of circumstances. Some of our stitchers are sometimes in a cell for 23 hours a day and yet produce impeccable highly-skilled work. We encourage them to realise a potential that they did not know they had and give them purpose to fulfil their lives via creativity,' adds Wendy.

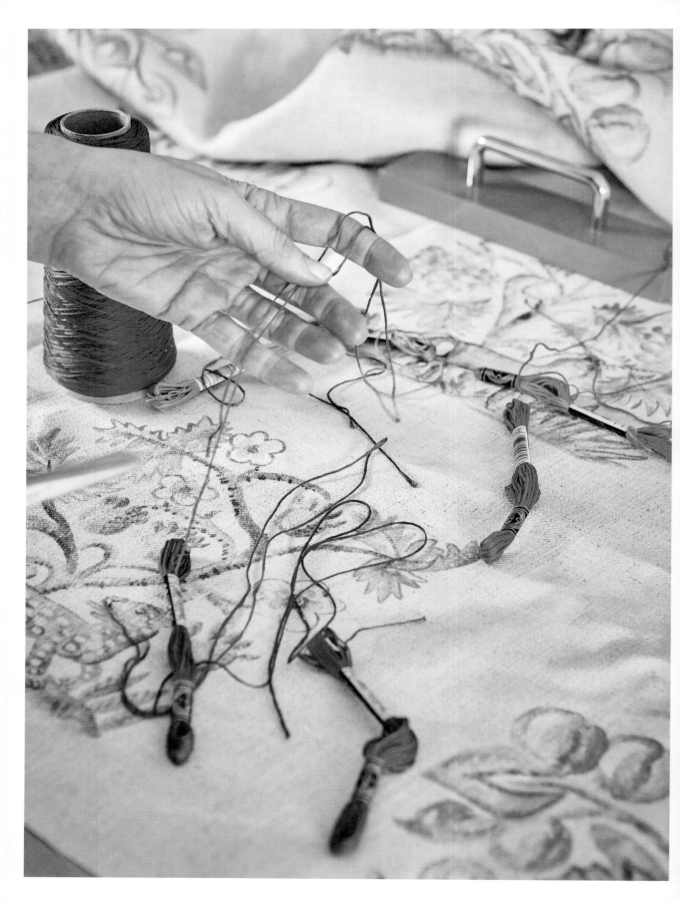

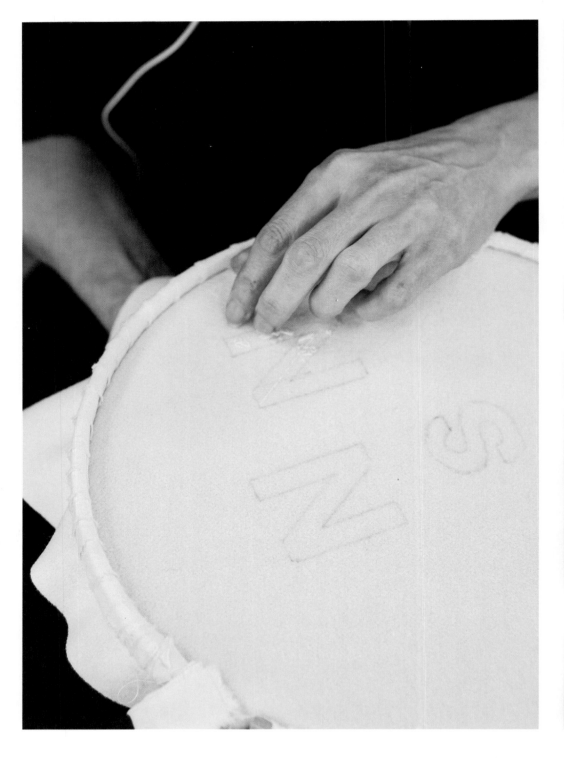

Decorator

LUCY HAMMOND GILES

London-born Lucy Hammond Giles is a Decorator at
Sibyl Colefax & John Fowler, the longest established
interior decorating firm in Great Britain and one of
the most respected in the world.

She has worked on and off for the company since first joining for
work experience 25 years ago, interspersed with stints in the film
and television industry and establishing her own design practice.
Lucy rejoined Sibyl Colefax & John Fowler in 2016 as a
full-time designer.

Inspired by the expertise and enthusiasm of colleagues, craftsmen
and clients, Lucy engages in commissions in a variety of styles.
Her elegant and low-key luxury approach to interiors has been
recently deployed in projects that include private houses in
London, the Cotswolds and the South of France.

LUCY HAMMOND GILES LIVES IN A
RED-BRICK HOUSE WITH HER HUSBAND
MARCO AND TWO SONS NEAR
LONDON'S LEAFY HOLLAND PARK.
THE LIVELY INTERIOR DESIGNER, OR
DECORATOR IN COLEFAX PARLANCE,
IS A LEADING TALENT AT ONE OF THE
GRAND DECORATING FIRMS.

Opening the front door to Lucy's house reveals a casually-stylish entrance hall and stairs to the first floor, which is tightly hung with art. Works by young artists like British painter Tim Garwood mingle with collections of things both inherited and accumulated with her husband. A painted dado visually links the ground floor to the upstairs. As a device the dado creates architectural interest and balances the visual weight of pictures displayed above. To the right, the living room is a work in progress.

A stream of diffused sunlight draws you into the largest room in the house, the kitchen/dining room. This open-plan room is dominated by a large bespoke bent wood bench (made by Matthew Bray) mimicking the curve of the oval Tulip dining table by Eero Saarinen; its size required craftsmen to build it in situ. 'The table was a present,' says Lucy. 'I did not choose it, it came to us and the bench was my response to this gift. If you are given a piece of furniture it makes you be more creative.'

On the shelving, cascading greenery, reference books and postcards share the limelight with special mementos, including a Mexican seated figure sculpture inherited from Lucy's step-grandfather. This combination of display and storage changes regularly. On the day of our visit, the installation included a hand-shaped mould used to make rubber gloves – 'my mother has something similar,' says Lucy – and beautiful things they've picked up as a family as well as pencils for Lucy and the children, 'in case we feel like doing some drawings.'

Behind the dining area is a space known to the family as the 'Quiz Room', where a campaign table from William James Antiques & Interiors sits in front of another comfortable banquette. Maps on the wall, a dart board and the children's art create a welcoming nook. 'I'm obsessed with maps, space and how things all fit together,' adds Lucy, 'and fascinated by the human body and how humans fit into our geography as well as in our interiors.' In this visual mix a peregrine falcon painted by one of her sons surveys cushions made from assorted fabrics, plus curtains in leftover 'Demedici' by Fortuny from Claremont. 'It was bought in the 1970s for a Colefax client but arrived a shade off and my mother bought the bolt. She was an assistant there in the 1970s,' she says, revealing a family connection to her current firm. 'The ticking, floral and leopard prints were my granny's cushions (the leopard had been the collar of a coat).' These disparate elements create a vibe that is full of character, playful and unselfconscious.

'I like the way our family uses our home,' adds Lucy. 'My husband has an office in the basement, we're all in the kitchen a lot and our bedrooms are on the first floor. The three-storey house is like a pyramid, small at the top and it gets bigger as you go down to the spacious lower ground level. It has a hidden depth.' She jokes about the layout, but indeed great thought has gone into all the layers of the interior.

'You gather things over time, and now that I'm over 40 I've woven my memories into our home and our stories as a family. I'm really proud of it, even though as a designer I know a lot of things are here because I don't yet have something better to replace them with,' explains Lucy. 'A lot of the artworks came from our parents' and grandparents' houses, and we have collected others together over the years. It's important to hang your art and have things up. My parents are divorced and growing up I always ended up moving things around from house to house to make my room my own. The reorganising of things made me feel safe. This house was a really good grounding after inhabiting my parents' homes and then boarding school. You make the most of what you've got.' Lucy certainly has.

'Other than the kitchen, my favourite room is the kids' bedroom on the first floor. It gets the morning light and I love the colours and the way they have made it their own. There was very little thought process behind it – it all just came together,' says Lucy. Initially, there was a bunk bed that has now been separated. Lucy wanted furniture that was suitable for children, which could be painted but that they can bash, and can grow with them. The separated beds are versatile and transformative and can one day become daybeds or comfortable sofas.

The rug was bought on a family holiday in Greece when Lucy was 17. 'It has never looked nice until now. I'm such a hoarder and this rug was just waiting for the right moment. The blind fabric is called "Rhubarb" by Jobs Handtryck; it is a triumph and goes with everything. I like the fact that boys can have floral printed textiles without the room looking too pretty. I've added botanical pictures. The floor cushions came from my mother.'

While the floors above ground are suffused with light, the moody lower ground floor surprises with a climbing wall and a comfortable escapist spare room. When guests come for a night they can enjoy this private refuge underground.

'People are sometimes surprised when they come into our house,' says Lucy. 'I did not want a basement and didn't want to dig one but in the end it was the best way to add space. I also wanted to make it fun for the boys. Marco and I often talk about Haruki Murakami's stories, and about going into other worlds and that being exciting. The hallway climbing wall was my husband's idea and I

worked on developing it so that it didn't look like a gym or a theme park. The background wall is stained plywood to soften it and it makes the holds look like sculptures, rather than something more utilitarian.

'The Eames' Lobby chair at the end of the hallway which belonged to decorators Tom Parr and then Wendy Nicholls came from Colefax after we moved from Brook Street to our new offices on the Pimlico Road. The patterned coir carpet from Sinclair Till was copied from my colleague Emma Burn's dining room.'

Off this hallway is the guest bedroom. 'I love it as it's a place of refuge and I wanted it to be comfortable,' says Lucy. There is a nod to detail in making disparate things fit together. The blue paint sets off the gilt picture frames, enhances the richness of the brown wood furniture and unifies the fabric choices. Lucy mixed the scale of textile patterns to create interest and balance. Having floral chintz makes the space feel fresh and yet it is not too sweet in this context. The more masculine antique pieces include a tallboy chest of drawers and caned-back chair which came from grandparents. Although this room is brand new it has a permanence which reveals the designer's deep knowledge of traditional interiors.

'To find inspiration I like going to old houses: National Trust houses (for example, architect John Soane's Pitzhanger Manor; Carlyle's House) are favourites, the Emery Walker Trust in Chiswick, and other people's houses. I usually drag the children because I think it's good for them. The more you can see from a young age the more you understand that there is no right or wrong way to live. There are just different ways to live,' says Lucy.

Lucy's style is elegant, comfortable, practical and relaxed – and this does not happen by accident. Walking around her house there is a

sense of proportion, learned from observing, as well as appreciating the relationship between one object and another. This relationship transcends style which is one of the reasons why the rooms in this house succeed regardless of how they are decorated.

'The key elements to an interior, in addition to good proportion, are having good light which makes you feel joyful; and ensuring that everything works for its intended purpose,' reveals Lucy. 'Our kitchen is where we spend most of our time. The space needed to be a kitchen, dining room and play room. The dining table needed to be not just for eating but also for sitting at. Our kitchen is more than utilitarian; it's a kids' play area shared with grown-ups. All has to be well considered and quite democratic as everyone has to be able to use it.'

Beyond the democratic Lucy's rooms are layered with older objects – whether from the 1970s or Georgian – that introduce a sense of timelessness. 'Why would you have something old?' she asks, and continues; 'Because they have stories – you need old things in an interior to add patina, texture, colour and layers; they also give variety to a room. Because they are bashed about, not perfect and not too clean in a nice way. A lack of perfection is very important. It's important not to be too precious. As soon as you have control you can let go.'

Interiors and Still Life Photographer

SARAH
HOGAN

Born in County Galway in Ireland, Sarah Hogan is a UK-based interiors and still life photographer. Having studied Mixed Media Art her work is known for its painterly use of light and the sense of calmness and clarity in her images.

With over 15 years' experience, Sarah shoots for established interior brands and collaborates with British and international publications, including *House & Garden*, *ELLE Decoration* and *Livingetc*. In addition to raising a young family, Sarah is also active in programmes that empower female photographers. Her images have been shortlisted for the Association of Photographers' Awards. She is thrilled to have just finished designing and building a new home with her entrepreneur husband in leafy Oatlands – to the south of London – that incorporates a new photography space.

HOW DO YOU DEFINE YOUR STYLE?

My style at home is a mix of modern and vintage with a focus on natural materials like birch, oak and marble. As a mother of three young children my husband and I strove to create a house that is both dramatic and easy to live in. In collaboration with our architect Wilkinson King we created an open, light-filled family home with plenty of storage and space for the kids to play.

WHAT SETS BRITISH DESIGN APART?

In my line of work I am lucky to be able to partner with and be exposed to a wide range of exciting contemporary design talent, from developers and their new projects to editors and product designers. British design is set apart by an attention to craftsmanship, combined with edge, by which I mean originality, quirkiness and personality. There is also an element of using new techniques in the creation of highly individual objects.

HOW IMPORTANT IS TECHNOLOGY IN YOUR WORK?

As a photographer I have had to embrace technology. I learned photography back in the days of film and fondly remember dropping the film at the lab. But as a commercial photographer I have to respond to my clients' needs and digital is the way we work now. I still shoot film for personal projects and often use my Polaroid 600 camera, which was the first camera I bought when I was 13.

ARE THERE ANY VISUAL RULES ANYMORE?

There is no right or wrong when it comes to your own home; it has more to do with your personality and how you want to live. Although some people are a little afraid to express themselves wildly at home, this is definitely changing. Rules are less important. I have become more confident in my choices knowing what I like, don't like and value.

In our house, we left the ceiling joists exposed, both as a feature and as an architectural trick to make the ceilings appear higher because you are not hiding the structural elements. For the house's exterior we used a custom mix of two different grey-coloured bricks to create a façade that is textured, less rigid and slightly softer in tone.

WHAT DO YOU MOST LIKE ABOUT YOUR HOME?

I have just moved into our current house so I'm still getting used to it. My husband and I have been on a long road to get to this point. First, we bought the flat under our old flat and combined both spaces. Then when we had twins and sold that, we bought a wreck of a late 1960s bungalow. One year in we realised it wasn't an option to 'do it up' and decided to knock it down and build a new house. It took another year to find the right architect – one who understood what we wanted and could work with us and our budget. Our requirements included making the most of our long narrow plot without losing the garden, designing a home on two levels and maximising the light, which is very important to me. It was all a little scary with twins, another baby on the way and our careers – but here we are having just completed our house!

I love the simplicity of the materials, the airiness of the space, the garden and the fact that the kids absolutely adore it. My favourite detail are the large windows looking out to old trees at the front of the property.

WHAT IS YOUR FAVOURITE CORNER OR ROOM AND WHY?

All of it. If I had to make a choice, I would say the bedroom because it's a (sort of) private room in the house just for my husband and me. It's an escape from the kids and it has a great view out to large ancient trees. We chose a landscape-shaped window to maximise the light in the room. The afternoon light is incredible because you get dappled moving shadows filtering through the leaves and branches outside.

We've kept the decor simple. The room is painted in a pale grey Dulux shade from their extensive colour palette because we didn't want the walls to be stark white. It's a warm and really subtle hue. Our bedding is linen topped with a silk and cotton throw from Essaouira in Morocco. The bed came from our previous house and it is a super king size so the kids can pile in. At the foot of the bed we placed a cork bench from Ikea. I love cork as a material and the kids sometimes climb on it to get into the bed.

WHAT MADE YOU WANT TO BECOME AN INTERIORS PHOTOGRAPHER?

I think that I am perhaps drawn to interiors because we moved so often as part of my dad's work. I always looked forward to painting my new room and making it mine. My dad was an amateur photographer so there were always cameras around. Maybe my choice of profession just happened naturally for me as a result of my interests and environment. My first jobs were assisting photographer Alex Wilson with whom I travelled a lot and also interiors photographer Bill Batten who contributes to *The World of Interiors* magazine.

As a photographer I feel privileged to work with and meet so many talented people – makers, designers, set designers, stylists, art directors; all those that help create the images that we see day to day and inspire us.

WHAT ARE THE KEY ELEMENTS OF A MODERN, PERSONAL AND STYLISH INTERIOR?

As someone who photographs a lot of interiors I'm always fascinated when I walk into someone's space. When I shoot I enjoy the spaces where you can see the person's character and how their life has evolved over time. This has nothing to do with a particular style but more about reflecting who they are.

I know everyone has different taste but to keep an interior modern I would try and keep it well edited, surrounding myself with things that are meaningful and useful. I would suggest adding lots of great family photos and enlarging some of the special ones. Inject some pattern and pops of colour with cushions and throws. My entrance hall, for example, has a green chair, blue throw and a patterned rug from John Lewis that is both graphic and practical.

Also try to incorporate as much good storage as possible to hide clutter as this certainly helps make a place look more stylish!

WHERE DO YOU FIND INSPIRATION?

All around. I try not to look at Pinterest or Instagram too much as there is so much to see and I can't focus on anything in particular. I like going to museums (the Wallace Collection and London's Design Museum), galleries (the National Portrait Gallery) and nature – places like Kew's Royal Botanic Gardens and RHS

Garden Wisley – all inspire my colour sense. I also find inspiration through reading novels (when I can with three kids under five).

HOW DO YOU SEE BRITISH DOMESTIC INTERIORS EVOLVING?

I see interiors getting more functional, personal and adapting to how we actually live as individuals. Our kitchen, for example, was designed to maximise storage and I wanted the kids to be able to play and run around the space. We purposely don't have a breakfast bar at the island so we can sit together around the dining table and eat our meals together.

When it came to designing the kitchen, my mother, who is a kitchen designer, had some good tips, such as going for darker colours for the doors to make the marble backsplash stand out as a feature, and smaller touches like the boiler tap which is amazing from a practical point of view.

WHAT ADVICE WOULD YOU GIVE SOMEONE ABOUT HOW TO BRING OUT THEIR OWN TASTE AND PERSONALITY?

Look at the things you love – whether art, photography or nature – and incorporate elements inspired by them in your home. Pay attention to your colour choices, even the most subtle shade can change a room. Paint is a really affordable way to try out some new ideas and experiment.

When it comes to fabric, a simple drape of beautiful fabric or a kimono hung on the wall can add real drama to a room with little effort. Remnants boxes in fabric shops are always a guilty pleasure of mine. If I'm ever in Soho or John Lewis I love buying fabrics which end up as cushions or backdrops in my shoots.

Designer

EMILIO
PIMENTEL-REID

Emilio Pimentel-Reid works across the disciplines of design, events, retail and publishing. Born in the Dominican Republic, Emilio studied fashion design at Parsons School of Design in New York. His love of colour and pattern developed at Oscar de la Renta, watching the designer mix seemingly unrelated fabrics and bold accessories, which combined to create the house's signature look. Emilio's understanding of clearly distilled visual concepts came from his formative time at Calvin Klein which led to an appreciation of minimalism.

A respect for both the contemporary and traditional later informed his move into the interiors field (following an MA and training in fine and decorative art at Sotheby's) at the cult American interiors magazine *Nest*, known for celebrating exceptional spaces and its bravery in valuing everything from igloos and prison cells to palaces.

Emilio launched his own multidisciplinary studio in 2012 following many years as the Decorating Editor at *ELLE Decoration* (UK). His range of commissions blends his interest in contemporary design and historic interiors with a sense of playfulness, rigour and a colourful aesthetic. He currently lives between London, south Somerset and the ancient city of Bath.

I MOVED TO BATH AFTER REDISCOVERING THE BEAUTIFUL CITY IN A MAGAZINE ARTICLE AT A TIME WHEN I WAS LOOKING FOR A CHANGE OF PERSPECTIVE.

Having outgrown my flat in west London and with many of my books already living in another property (a hexagonal folly in south Somerset), I longed for a home within easy train access to the capital and a short drive to my country escape. The gorgeous ancient city of Bath, which saw growth as a fashionable spa town in the eighteenth century, is like a theatre set that delights even in the rain when I walk downhill to the train station for my early-morning London commute.

Spread across the two main floors of a Grade I listed Regency building, I now enjoy a sun-filled duplex with high ceilings, architectural details that survived the blitz and creaking floorboards of Baltic pine. The front overlooks the handsome chestnut trees of one of the first public parks in the country, and the back my romantically overgrown garden.

Designed by architect John Pinch the elder in 1815, the rooms have been restored and updated for modern life by the team at Donald Insall Associates. The clear light and airiness of the apartment reminds me of growing up in the Dominican Republic surrounded by lush vegetation and high glass-paned windows.

I have reimagined my flat as an indulgent one bedroom with a living room, library/home office, as well as a kitchen (in the former withdrawing room) and a garden room.

The flat is a fun work in progress as I am slowly decorating it in between work trips, photoshoots and community activism. My favourite room is the living room, which I've painted in a pink hue mixed to complement my skin tone by the talented artisans at Little Greene. Specialists advise that you paint your space in a colour that suits the room (which is true) – and I hope I have done – but actually why not also deploy a colour that flatters the homeowner? The rug, which is worn just the way I like it, was found by dealer friend Patrick Macintosh and came from the Fonthill Estate. I love that the rug helps anchor the room and keeps the pink from looking too pretty.

I've reupholstered the two 1960s sofas in an oatmeal-coloured linen from Romo and slipcovered them in a cotton stripe from British brand Fermoie which allows me to change the look of the room. They actually belonged to the previous owner and wanting to avoid the hassle of finding new ones when these already had the right scale, I bought them from her and transformed them with my preferred fabrics. The blue cushions are in a Howard Hodgkin-designed fabric by Designers Guild and the other ones came from Turkey. The 1970s brass coffee table from Brown Rigg in Gloucestershire and other furniture has come to me over the years. The Gothic plant stand by the window made for an Irish rectory was spotted at Battersea's Decorative Antiques & Textiles Fair. It did not sell and I later hunted it down from the dealer at a better price.

I often work on my laptop at the round Regency table by the window sitting on an African throne or Ashanti stool. I've loved this style since my days in New York working for Cuban–American interior designer Vicente Wolf who often used similar ones in his projects. I'm also a big fan of the 1980s Memphis movement and the 'Shogun' striped floor lamp is by Swiss architect Mario Botta. The Regency chairs are in a favourite fabric from Italian textile house Dedar. As a stylist my flat keeps changing, and I am due any day to take some pieces out of storage in New York to give my interior a more finished look. In the meantime, I bring in flowers from the garden and keep adding finds.

I enjoy discovering new design across the UK, and I blend contemporary design I like with antiques – from Georgian to the nineteenth-century Aesthetic Movement and 1930s Heal's pieces. I shift accessories around usually on a daily basis, which is probably why I've ended up as an editor and stylist.

Although I have a degree in Economics I always knew that I would not be working in finance (although I don't rule out politics). My mother, who has a sharp eye, subscribed to what seemed like every magazine when I was growing up and perhaps set me on the editorial path. After graduation I enrolled at Parsons School of Design in New York for a degree in Fashion Design and I later moved to London to study for my MA in Fine and Decorative Art at Sotheby's London, which opened my eyes to all the different art and design collecting categories available. I like to call this my shopping degree.

Working freelance as an Interiors Specialist I get to be involved with a range of projects, from offering style, trend and colour direction for brands, to the interiors I have lately started decorating for private clients in the UK and abroad. Inspiration really does come from everywhere, not because everything is inspiring but because over the years you learn to see. Attending fairs, student shows and auction previews, and seeing lots of things there, you tune out the irrelevant and focus on what is special and interesting. I'm still learning lots and asking questions, which helps me keep moving and expands my design horizons.

My style at home is personal and reflects my interests, upbringing, friendships and mentors. I'm exposed to and work with the most contemporary things in my professional life and yet don't want to live exclusively surrounded by newness. I appreciate furniture with history, and having a couple of pieces dating from the same period as the building show what the interior could have looked like in the past. They also look great in the context for which they were created. I live with a mix of Georgian, Regency and Victorian furniture as well as pieces that have just been launched. Colour and pattern make me happy and the scale of my rooms (the ceilings are over 4.5 metres/15 feet high) means I have the challenge of plenty of wall space to hang art and textiles. I don't care about price or provenance in the sense that something good does not need to be expensive. I regularly pick up fabrics, ceramics and many other interesting accessories at vintage shops and local markets. Other times I do fall for more expensive things that require a little more consideration before I invest.

My preference at home is for furniture and accessories that are well made and not disposable – whether old or new. If I really love something, I'm not afraid to go for a trendy piece; I know the trend will eventually be forgotten and I will end up with an object that I love forever.

In my library/home office, which I use more to relax than for work, I've painted the walls a mineral green colour specially mixed by Papers and Paints in Chelsea. The comfortable linen sofa I've had for years, while the Regency daybed has been refreshed with a zigzag fabric from Borderline in paprika red. The gold stool is by British design duo Fredrikson Stallard – I found it many years ago at the David Gill Gallery stand at PAD, London's fair for twentieth-century art and design. I had the runner made from Spanish wool grain sacks and the metal folding table came from my old apartment in New York. I try not to throw things out. The herringbone pattern seagrass flooring from Alternative Flooring feels great underfoot and visually links this room to my bedroom next door creating a comfortable relaxing suite.

History is very important in my field and as an editor I approach every object or new design

with a knowledge of what came before and an understanding of the influences that may have inspired it. This allows me to build up a context against which to compare and assess what I am looking at. When I write about design or judge a new product in a graduate show, my knowledge of the past helps me draw out an object's story, its originality, quality and relevance. When it comes to styling and creating interiors, I cannot get enough of visiting historic houses and well-designed rooms that I may have access to for inspiration.

Not being trained as an interior or product designer I am not someone who follows rules. I go by what my eye tells me feels right. This approach probably comes from having an interest in rooms and how people live. There are certainly elements of balance, proportion and comfort to consider. In my bedroom the antique brass bed (by Hoskins & Sewell which supplied the White Star Line) is titanic in scale so that it doesn't get dwarfed by the room's dimensions. To keep it from looking too trad I've balanced it with a drum stool from Conran's Habitat bought at a vintage shop in Connecticut, and a contemporary reading lamp from Flos propped up by books to achieve the right height. The quilt was a Christmas gift from the Anthropologie PR team. On the back wall are Haitian paintings bought at the market in Santo Domingo and the wing chair is from my New York apartment re-upholstered in a textured Manuel Canovas plum-coloured linen. The pale blue walls – a Mylands paint – create a calming backdrop to wake up to.

To me the key element of a successful interior is having a point of view and sticking to it. When I used to commission stylists at *ELLE Decoration*, I always asked them to write in one line what their shoot idea was about. This one-liner helped focus attention on a clear theme and everything else could flow from there.

As a British citizen who was born elsewhere I find that design in the UK is full of energy, personality and possibility. Our designers take risks and are commercially successful, but commerce is not usually the starting point. British design spring from ideas, stories, historical skills and craft. At the moment, British interiors are evolving in varied directions and they are all valid. Whether modern, clean and hyper-edited, traditional or colourful, many of us are looking to break free from prescribed concepts of how we should live. At a time when we are bombarded with so many images, product choices and possibilities it can be extremely difficult to narrow down one's style. I suggest regularly disconnecting from social media to explore historic rooms and books from other decades for inspiration. Take a look at furniture layouts, colours, textures and discover what feels right to you. Chances are that if something still looks good after decades or centuries it's something worth being inspired by today.

When I wrote my MA dissertation at the beginning of my career, I focused on the nineteenth-century taste instruction manuals (the precursors to today's design magazines and blogs), which attempted to educate the nascent middle classes on the concept of taste. They all started by saying that taste was about your own personality and then proceeded to tell the reader what that should be. I'm glad we are no longer living in that age and are free to explore our individual creativity, as I hope the varied interiors and styles in this book will attest.

ADDRESS BOOK

Although far from an exhaustive list, here are some of our – and the featured designers' – top British style resources to help you get started on your own bold British interior.

ANTIQUES

Brown Rigg *brownrigg-interiors.co.uk*

Christopher Howe *howelondon.com*

Jack Laver Brister *tradchap.com*

Lorfords *lorfordsantiques.com*

Macintosh Antiques *macintoshantiques.co.uk*

Max Rollitt *maxrollitt.com*

Rose Uniacke *roseuniacke.com*

Sibyl Colefax & John Fowler *sibylcolefax.com*

ANTIQUE AND VINTAGE MARKETS, AND FAIRS

Ardingly IACF (International Antiques & Collectors Fairs) *iacf.co.uk/ardingly*

Builth Wells International Antiques and Collectors Fair *continuityfairs.co.uk/builth-wells*

Decorative Antiques & Textiles Fair *decorativefair.com*

Midcentury Modern Vintage and Contemporary Interior Show *modernshows.com*

Portobello Market *portobelloroad.co.uk/the-market*

Shepton Flea *sheptonflea.com*

Sunbury Antiques Market, Kempton *sunburyantiques.com/kempton*

ART AND PRINTS

Bjorn Rune Lie *bjornlie.com*

Camilla Perkins *camillaperkins.com*

Jesse Collett *jessecollett.co.uk*

Hester Finch *partnershipeditions.com*

Paul Catherall *paulcatherall.com*

Romily Hay *romilyhay.com*

Sarah Graham *grahamgallery.co.uk*

AUCTION HOUSES

Bonhams *bonhams.com*

Christie's *christies.com*

Phillips *phillips.com*

Sotheby's *sothebys.com*

CERAMICS

Hitomi Hosono *hitomihosono.com*

Portmeirion *portmeirion.co.uk*

Wedgwood *wedgwood.co.uk*

DESIGN AND DECORATIVE ART

Adrian Sassoon *adriansassoon.com*

Bethan Gray *bethangray.com*

David Gill Gallery *davidgillgallery.com*

Fredrikson Stallard *fredriksonstallard.com*

The New Craftsmen *thenewcraftsmen.com*

Sebastian Cox *sebastiancox.co.uk*

Thomas Messel *thomasmessel.com*

Yinka Ilori *yinkailori.com*

DESIGN FAIRS AND SHOWROOMS

Affordable Art Fair *affordableartfair.com*

Chelsea Design Quarter
chelseadesignquarter.co.uk

Clerkenwell Design Week
clerkenwelldesignweek.com

Collect *craftscouncil.org.uk*

Decorative Antiques & Textiles Fair
decorativefair.com

Decorex *decorex.com*

Design Week and Focus at Design Centre
Chelsea Harbour *dcch.co.uk*

Frieze *frieze.com/fairs/frieze-london*

London Design Fair *londondesignfair.co.uk*

Masterpiece *masterpiecefair.com*

Pavilion of Art and Design (PAD)
pad-fairs.com/london

Pimlico Road *thepimlicoroad.com*

FLOORING AND RUGS

Alternative Flooring *alternativeflooring.com*

Christopher Farr *christopherfarr.com*

HARDWARE

Pinxton & Co *pinxtonandco.com*

HISTORIC HOUSES

English Heritage *english-heritage.org.uk*

National Trust *nationaltrust.org.uk*

National Trust for Scotland *nts.org.uk*

HOTELS

Firmdale Hotels *firmdalehotels.com*

INTERIORS

Collett–Zarzycki *collett-zarzycki.com*

Emilio Pimentel-Reid *pimentel-reid.com*

Sibyl Colefax & John Fowler *sibylcolefax.com*

KITCHEN

Konig Kitchens *konigkitchens.com*

Rossi Stone Surfaces *rossistoneworks.com*

LIGHTING

Alexandra Robinson Design
alexandrarobinson.com

Marianna Kennedy *mariannakennedy.com*

Melodi Horne *melodihorne.com*

Original BTC *originalbtc.com*

Plumen *plumen.com*

MIRRORS

English Georgian *englishgeorgian.com*

MUSEUMS

National Portrait Gallery *npg.org.uk*

Natural History Museum *nhm.ac.uk*

The Design Museum, London *designmuseum.org*

Victoria & Albert (V&A) *vam.ac.uk*

Victoria & Albert Dundee *vam.ac.uk/dundee*

Wallace Collection *wallacecollection.org*

The Wedgwood Museum
wedgwoodmuseum.org.uk

Tate *tate.org.uk*

PAINT

Farrow & Ball *farrow-ball.com*

Little Greene *littlegreene.com*

Mylands *mylands.com*

Paint & Paper Library *paintandpaperlibrary.com*

Papers and Paints *papersandpaints.co.uk*

PHOTOGRAPHY

Sarah Hogan *sarahhoganphoto.com*

PROFESSIONAL BODIES

Walpole Group *thewalpole.co.uk*

RETAIL

The Conran Shop *conranshop.co.uk*

Habitat *habitat.co.uk*

Harrods *harrods.com*

Heal's *heals.com*

Liberty *libertylondon.com*

Petra Palumbo *petrapalumbo.com*

SILVERSMITH

Hal Messel *halmessel.com*

TEXTILES AND WALLPAPER

Borderline *borderlinefabrics.com*

Cole & Son *cole-and-son.com*

Designers Guild *designersguild.com*

Dyeworks *dyeworks.co.uk*

Fromental *fromental.co.uk*

Fermoie *fermoie.com*

Fine Cell Work *finecellwork.co.uk*

Little Greene *littlegreene.com*

Manuel Canovas *manuelcanovas.com*

Mini Moderns *minimoderns.com*

Morris & Co *stylelibrary.com/morris&co*

Romo *romo.com*

Sibyl Colefax & John Fowler *sibylcolefax.com*

Tori Murphy *torimurphy.com*

Zoffany *stylelibrary.com/zoffany*

TILES

Fired Earth *firedearth.com*

A WORD OF THANKS

EMILIO PIMENTEL-REID

I would first like to thank the designers whose houses and studios are shown in this book. The delight I receive from your work inspires me daily to collaborate with talented people and champion British design.

This book would not have been possible without the beautiful images shot by my co-author Sarah Hogan. Her sensitive photography captures both the authenticity and subtlety of these interiors.

The following individuals deserve great credit for the creation of *Bold British Design*: Sarah Lavelle, Publishing Director at Quadrille, who commissioned the book; and Claire Rochford and Emily Lapworth, whose graphic ingenuity helps tell our stories. I could not have asked for a better editor than the gracious Imogen Fortes and thank her for her energy, stimulus and reassurance.

A big thank you to my assistants Roxanne Gaunt and Bethan Reen.

To all my clients as well as my colleagues at *Nest* magazine and *ELLE Decoration* as well as the many talented individuals at British *GQ*, international editions of *Architectural Digest* and *The Sunday Times Style* with whom I've had the pleasure to work.

There are other important people I should thank who have had great influence over my life: DJRC, CTR, GTO, CRF, ERF, MCO and *especially* GRT.

Likewise, I owe so much to my mentors Mark Casertano, Joseph Holzman and Vicente Wolf, without whose individual vision, creativity and sprinkling of magic and encouragement at different stages of my professional life I would not have discovered my world of interiors.

To my friends José Ramón Reyes, Mark Tennyson-d'Eyncourt and Marc Spidelman, who put up with my extravagances and who are always there for brainstorming ideas.

And finally to JLD, who accompanies me on this adventure every day.

SARAH HOGAN

I would like to start by thanking Emilio as this book started with the two of us brainstorming ideas over tea a number of years back. It was such a privilege to have worked on this book with you Emilio – thank you for all your positivity and encouragement. I am listed as co-author however Emilio is the true author; his words take us on an immense journey through the homes and studios of our tastemakers. Together, we have brought this book to life and I couldn't be prouder. We had some fun road trips, visits to florists and hotel stays on our UK tour.

Sarah Lavelle and Claire Rochford: thank you for your support with this book. Emily Lapworth, you are a superstar! Having your knowledge, eye for detail and design was a privilege. Imogen, for helping us guide the words and keeping us in check; I am incredibly grateful. Thank you to all at Quadrille for this amazing opportunity.

As a mother of three kids under five, I couldn't have physically shot this book without the continued support of my husband James, Grandma Mary and Renata. You all helped look after the twins, taking them to school and looking after Minnie, my firecracker toddler. I hope that one day my trio will pick this up and see what can be achieved if you work hard and do what you love.

I couldn't not thank some of the photographers whom I assisted years back and encouraged me on the path to becoming a photographer. Alex Wilson and Bill Batten: as well as technical skills, you taught me to be true to myself and love what I do. All my clients, art directors and stylists I have worked with, I am grateful.

Lastly but certainly not least, thank you to everyone featured in the book. We were so fortunate to be able to see inside the homes and studios of some of the most talented people working in interiors and design in the UK. Thank you to all of you for the coffees, cakes and lunches you provided and for allowing us in and showing us your spaces, creative ideas and homes.

CREDITS

We have made every effort to contact and credit all the makers, artists and designers whose work appears incidentally in the book and will be more than happy to correct listings or add any omissions in future reprints.

GUY TOBIN

Kitchen Photograph *Twin Manicurists* from the 'Incarnations' series by Janieta Eyre; 'Rook', graphite on paper, 65x55cm, 2013 by Chris Otley; Teapot by Emma Bridgewater; Tiles *Casino Baccarat* by www. firedearth.com.

Living Room 1950s' Italian mirror attributed to Fontana Arte; Right Angle Wall light in dark bronze by Rose Uniacke; Plaster pendant by Alexandra Robinson, inspired by Chester Jones; Sofa fabric by Leliévre Paris; Cushion in *Beautiran* by www.bennisonfabrics.com; Cushion by Fine Cell Work; Etching *Head of Ali*, 1999 by Freud, Lucian 1922-2011 / Private Collection / © The Lucian Freud Archive / Bridgeman Images; Four small artworks by Unknown artist working in Rome during WWII; Artworks by Romily Hay; The 'Semainier' by Rose Uniacke.

Study Blue swirl cups by David Garland; Plates by Roger Law; Brass Mechanical Piano Stool designed by CH Hare & Son. Late 19th century.

Baby's room Lithograph by Sarah Graham; Painting by Ralston Gudgeo 1910-1984; Paintings by Gerald Leslie Brockhurst: *Aglaia* (Anais), 1926 (a), *La Tresse* (Anais), October 1926 (b), *Mélisande* (Anais), also known as *Head of a Girl*, July 1920 (c), all © Richard Woodward; Curtains in *Aztec* by www.bennisonfabrics.com.

Girl's room Etching *Untitled (Rabbit)*, 2005 by Oliver Clegg; Headboard in *Faded Cinnabar* by Bennison Fabrics; Cushion in *Beautiran* by www.bennisonfabrics.com; Lampshade by Romily Hay; Linocut *Sasha* by Richard Bawden; Screenprint *Pet* by Sam3, www. sam3.es; Print *Tree Of Life* by Degreestore.net; Print by Swedish artist Einar Hansen 1932; *Poster Tsunami Relief* by Daniel Freytag, Instagram @madebyfolk.

Master Bedroom Roman Blind in *Treescape* by www.bennisonfabrics. com; Painting by Claudia Massie; Pillow case in *Liliana* by www. bennisonfabrics.com; Painting by Tim Scott Bolton, Oman; Two engravings from the description de l'Egypte ou recueil des observations et des recherches qui ont été faits en Egypte pendant l'expédition de l'armée française. 1809 - 1813; Lamps by LE KLINT A/S, Denmark.

CAMILLA PERKINS

Living room Paintings by Hester Finch, courtesy of www. partnershipeditions.com; Print *Flowers of Evil* by Bjorn Rune Lie, www.bjornlie.com; Cushion by Bungalow; Candlestick by Fair trade & Sustainable Homewares, Ian Snow, www.iansnow.com; Vase by Ben Sutton; Orange glass vase and plant pot by Garden Trading, www. gardentrading.co.uk; Art created by Ryan Rhodes and Caleb Everitt of Land.

Kitchen Exhibition Poster Africa - Architecture, Culture and Identity 25.06 - 25.10.15, artwork used is by J.D, 'Okhai Ojeikere: Online Gogoro Or Akaba, 1975; Tablecloth by Camilla Perkins; Alphabet brush pots by Bridie Hall; Oven gloves by Bespoke Binny - Natalie Manima; Toy car http://www.retroroller.eu/nl.

Stairs Power Poster, Painting of fish and artwork of letter P all by Camilla Perkins; 'V&A exhibition poster by Frida Kahlo: Making Her Self Up/ Image: *Frida on the bench*, 1939, photograph by Nickolas Muray (detail) © Nickolas Muray Photo Archives.

Bedroom Painting by Camilla Perkins; Blanket by Nicki Trench.

HITOMI HOSONO Artist's own

KEITH STEPHENSON AND MARK HAMPSHIRE

Living room Sofa's by Robin and Lucienne Day Foundation; Pavilion cushion by Mini Moderns; World's Fair Circus Glass New York 1964-1965; Button & Badge Map of the British Isles, by Hello Geronimo; Rug by Alternative Flooring, 01264 335111, www.alternativeflooring. com; Poster 'Design' from The Council of Industrial Design, March 1956 from Surface View; Lamp on shelf by Tom Dixon; Table lamp by Anglepoise; Bronzed cast resin vintage lamp base in the style of Robert Phandeve; Arabia enamelware bowl "Ritari" by Raija Uosikkinen. Finel & Arabia / Wärtsilä; String Shelving System.

Designed by Nisse&Kajsa Strinning, 1949. Producer: String Furniture AB, Malmö, Sweden. www.stringfurniture.com.

Dining room Newgate Pluto Sunburst Wall Clock, www. newgateworld.com; Vintage sideboard Kofod-Larsen by G-Plan; Mogens Kold danish dining set by Arne Hovmand Olsen; Vitra Eames RAR Rocking Chair/ Eames® chairs are designed by Charles and Ray Eames.

Studio The Old Futurist theatre in Scarborough by Keith Stephenson.

Office Portmeirion Totem teapot, the image has been reproduced with the kind permission of Portmeirion Group UK Limited, to whom all rights are reserved; Beryl Ware from Woods; Gorilla figures by Jamie Hewlett and Kid Robot; Darjeeling ceramics by Mini Moderns; Table by Unto this last.

Bedroom Beside lamps by Anglepoise; Furniture designed by Mini Moderns and Charles McKenzie; Lino print by 'Goldfinger I' ,www. paulcatherall.com; Mug by Holkham Pottery; Vase by Habitat, www. habitat.co.uk; Birthday card in frame by James Ross.

BETHAN GRAY Artist's own

NICOLAS ROOPE

Dining room Leather vintage chairs, *The Handy* formerly known as 'NV31' chair (1956) of Kai Kristiansen; Starman vase, Diesel Living with Seletti; Decode Vessel lampshade by Plumen with Plumen 002 bulb; Dining table 'SM74' made in Denmark by Skovby; Wine rack by Habitat, www.habitat.co.uk.

Living room Chair by Bertoia Diamond Chair by Harry Bertoia 1952 by Knoll; Calendar by Stendig, designed by Massimo Vignelli, 1966 and Published by Cromwell Company (Nashville, TN, USA); Table lamp by Rob Gijsbers en Jan Melis - Planet Amsterdam; Mirina Rug by Linie Design; Prints by Kitty McCall; Monkey by Kay Bojesen.

Bedroom Brass Drop Hat shade by Plumen; Plumen 001 bulb.

GEORGIA COLLETT

External shot Alexandra and Ainsworth Estate with permission from the A&A TRA.

Living room Large portrait by Jesse Collett; Face Print on shelf by David Champion; Colour block painting by David Hood; Flowers in Vase prints by Marco Del Re/ Galerie Maeght, Paris; Afridans stool by Christian Astuguevieille from Holly Hunt; Geomentric cushion by Conran Shop; Lampshade by Caravane; 'Assemble Stripe' rug by Collett-Zarzycki for Christopher Farr; Foot stool from sofa.com; Sofa from Sofa.com; Table lamps by Ilse Crawford for Ikea Sinnerlig range.

Kitchen Print *Battersea Blue IV* by www.paulcatherall.com; Minature paintings by David Hood; Teak Dining set by Tom Robertsons for A.H McIntosh Furniture.

Bedroom Pillow and fabric on headboard Cymbeline by Tibor Reich 1951; Monoprints by Georgia Collett; Forsa bedside lamp by Ikea.

HAL MESSEL

Kitchen Paintings: *Theatre Costume Design* and *Charmaine Scott* all Oliver Messel; Dining chairs by Thomas Messel.

Living room York Sofas; Ercol sofa upholstered in White Mali Mudcloth fabric and cushions by www.nomaddesign.co.uk; Painting *The Holy Family with the Infant St John* by Sir Joshua Reynolds 1788–9; Paintings: *Girl with Flower, Girl with Camera, Study* and *Miss Barbado*s, all Oliver Messel; Still life by Pepe Messel; Painted tile taken from the William Kipp engraving of Bradley Court, by Pepe Messel; Lamp, Crucifixion woodcut, Giant wax clam shells all Oliver Messel; Carved griffin and Gilt sconces by Thomas Messel.

Office/Drawing room Red chairs Lord Snowdon design for the 1969 investiture of Prince Wales at Caernarfon Castle; Bookcase by Thomas Messel; Silver goblets by Hal Messel.

Bedroom Framed costume designs for Sleeping beauty and Portrait of Designer Carolina Herrera by Oliver Messel; Beside lights by Billy Baldwin.

SEB COX

Collection of Bespoke furniture by Seb Cox, made from British wood in the showroom and studio in Greenwich, London, with the exclusion of Pit fired pottery by Elliott Ceramics, www.elliottceramics. com and Teapot by Sue Pryke.

LIZZIE DESHAYES

Main room Shimla wallpaper, Screen in custom Blood Olive Nonsuch design, Vintage day bed and cushion in Ukiyo-e design on velvet, Vintage day bed in Carapace design, Cushions in handpainted Bamboo design on velvet, Cherry Blossom design on velvet, Bonaparte design on velvet, all by Fromental; Blue sofa by sofa.com; Buttoned Stool by George Smith; Chair reupholstered by Franklin Upholstery www.franklinupholstery.co.uk; Table by Dessin Fournir; Lamp shade by Lizzie Deshayes.

Dining Paradis Vase by Raynaud Porcelain and Fromental; Nonsuch panel, Bruyere wallpaper (inspired by the work of Jean Lurçat) and Nimbus wallpaper all by Fromental; Light by Best and Lloyd; Table by Dessin Fournir; Tankha painting by artist at Fromental; Handpainted vase commissioned in China by Fromental.

Studio Bookcase by William Warbrick Furniture; Plates Hen and Chicks and Feed the Dog by Lizzie Deshayes; Painting Les Boas by Fromental.

YINKA ILORI

Artist's own and Face print *Tender Lines* by Lynnie Z, 2018; Clock by Braun *BC17*.

PETER GOMEZ

Living Room Jensen dining table by Westelm; Exhibition poster *Dirty Words Pictures* by Gilbert and George at the Serpentine Gallery; Jekca Cat by Jekca U.K. Limited, www.jekca.uk, @jekcauk; Lampshade by Ikea; Woodblock print by India Rose Bird, www.indiarosebird.com/indiarosebird@gmail.com; Photograph by Matthew; Zoffany fabrics: Verdi Velvet, Kuba zinc, 'Abstract 1928' from Icons Collection, KUBA Lapis, BRIK tigers eye, Atticus Garnet and Verdi Appliqué; *Noota, Verdi Damask* Velvet. Bargello Rug by Zoffany;

Bedroom *Richmond Park* wallpaper, *Ozias - Poison* fabric, *Garrick* wool blanket, and artwork all by Zoffany; Metal cabinets and light by Ikea; Exterior shot, Brentford dock flats designed by Sir Roger Walter in 1968.

MELINA BLAXLAND-HORNE Designer's own

RUTH MOTTERSHEAD

Bedroom Framed William Morris Fritillary wallpaper, from 1885 - Morris & Co.; Lamp by Ikea; Liberty fabric cushions;

Guest Bedroom Wallpaper Abbey Gardens by Paint and Paper Library; Side table by Ikea; Bed by Made.com; Cushion by Wesley Barrell.

Snug Print by William Morris; Lamp by John Lewis & Partners, www.johnlewis.com; Sofa by Ikea; Chair by Made.com; Blind by www.clarke-clarke.com Stockists on our website; Wallpaper Carlton House Terrace by Little Greene; Cushion in Sanderson fabric.

Living room Sofa by Sofa Workshop; Rug and side table by Ikea; Curtains by www.clarke-clarke.com, Stockists on our website; Sukoshi Small Lidded Seagrass Basket Black by ALSO Home www.alsohome.com.

MINNIE KEMP

Studio Print *Giselle: Glimpse*, by Eileen Cooper 2017; Chair by Holland & Sherry; Moodboard: *Subway Riders*, Ralph Fasanella (1950), New York City, United States 1917–1997, oil on canvas, 28 x 60 in; American Folk Art Museum, gift of Ralph and Eva Fasanella, 1995.8.1. Photo by Adan Reich; winter invitation (fireplace) by Rachael Cocker at 8 Holland Street. Beads by Margit Wittig and www.margitwittig.com; Orange fabric by Ardmore designs; Set of 30 prints of an antique (17th/18th Century) astrological/cosmological map framed by Marcus Wells; Toile De Jouy tea towel framed by Marcus Wells, Haviland designs.

Hotel room Curtains in Mulberry fabric; Uphosterd chairs in Embroidery Indiana fabric by Pierre Frey and fabrics supplied by Abbott & Boyd; artwork by Peter Clark, peterclarkcollage.com; Mirror by Andrew Martin; Light by Kit Kemp; Footstool in fabrics supplied by Abbott & Boyd; Hand Carved Table, Chelsea Textiles for Kit Kemp; Back of chair Pierre Frey – Embroidered "ORIGINES" fabric (inspired from a traditional Kenyan skirt); Yellow chair in fabrics supplied by Abbott & Boyd. Mont Blanc Daffodil leather by Moore & Giles; Rug by Tim Page; Sofa in fabrics supplied by Abbott & Boyd.

CHARLIE BOWLES

Living room Original BTC lights: Chester Floor Light/Oxford Double Table Light/Hatton 3 Floor Light/Pembridge size 3 pendant; A4 Regency Convex Mirror, www.englishgeorgian.com; Cushion by Tori Murphy Fastnet Stripe, Cadogan Check cushions, www.torimurphy.

com Tel: 01773 711 128; Steiff Lion; Rug by The Rug Company, www.therugcompany.com; Cushion by Marianne Diemer, Textile Designer, Rouge du Rhin; A24 Irish Peat Bucket, www.englishgeorgian.com; Brissi velvet armchair; Sofa and Pouffe by sofa.com; Amethyst Glass Vase by Evitavonni.

Kitchen Original BTC Fin Horizontal pendant; The Spline Chairs and Oskar table were designed by Sean Dare for Dare studio; Salt and Pepper designed by Peter Bowles, manufactured and sold in the early 1990s; Glassware from BTC's glass factory - English antique glass, handblown by Walter.

Bedroom Original BTC lights: Pembridge size 3 pendant/Fin Wall Light; Painting by Julia Bowles; Bed by Feather and Black; Climbing Chevy cushion, and Fastnet Stripe throw by Tori Murphy/www.torimurphy.com; Vito Stool and Kingston Dressing Table by Sean Dare for Dare Studio; Pouffe by Design House Stockholm; Wooden Tray by John Lewis & Partners, www.johnlewis.com.

FINE CELL WORKS

Wandsworth Cushion by Charlene Mullen; Cushion by Blithfield and Kit Kemp Circles; Fabric by Kit Kemp for Andrew Martin Hedgerow Fabric; Cushion by Cressida Bell Shield; Tango Cushion by Neisha Crosland.

LUCY HAMMOND GILES

Kitchen Saarinen Dining Table by Knoll; Maria Light by Urban Cottage Industries, www.urbancottageindustries.com; Watercolour by Philip Hooper; Bird plate by John Derain; Plaster sconce by Peter Hone for Pentreath & Hall; The Comfort of Food series by Tony Scherman; Papyrus lampshade by Robert Kime; High Upholstered Bar Stool in Brass by Rose Uniacke; Blue chair by Tripp Trapp® ; Chair by Vintage Poul Nørreklit chair from Sigmar; Fez Weave Cushions in Peacock from the Guy Goodfellow Collection. guygoodfellowcollection.com; Cushion, curtain and blind by Fortuny.

Kids room Blind fabric by Jobs Handtryck Sweden, Gocken Jobs, Rabarber, 1968; Red Lamp by Habitat, www.habitat.co.uk; Original BTC Hector light.

Staircase Painting by Tim Garwood; Print of original NASA photo from Apollo 8 Mission, December 1963 from Themes and Variations; Elisabeth Lecourt London map from Les Robes Géographiques;

Basement Bedroom Photograph by Khaled Kassem; Paintings *Slate Rocks Valentina (County Kerry)* and *The Breakwater, Porlock Wier* by EW Cooke 1811-1880; Birds sampler from Barbie Campbell Cole; Stripe Curtain fabric from Claremont.

Basement Conran tube lights; Poster by Lauren Baker, www.laurenbakerart.com; Painting by EW Cooke1811-1880; Eames® chairs are designed by Charles and Ray Eames; Painting by Vera Southby.

SARAH HOGAN

Bedroom Bed by Warren Evans; Cork Bench by Ikea; Bedside lamp by flos; Photography bt Sarah Hogan; Flooring by Flooring by Atkinson & Kirby / www.akirby.com; Screen print by Woodstock Artist association.

Kitchen DSW Eames® chairs are designed by Charles and Ray Eames; Table Legs by Habitat, www.habitat.co.uk; Table top by Ikea; Rug in kitchen by H&M Home.

Hall Rug in by John Lewis & Partners, www.johnlewis.com; Serigraph poster for Doris Lee memorial exhibition at the WAAM.

EMILIO PIMENTEL-REID

Sitting room Sofa upholstered in York Stripe by Fermoie. www.fermoie.com; Cushion covers in 'Brush' fabric by Howard Hodgkin for Designers Guild , www.designersguild.com; Floor Lamp 'Shogun' by Mario Botta; Regency chairs covered in fabric by Dedar; Desk lamp 1228 by Anglepoise.

Library Seagrass flooring by Alternative Flooring, www.alternativeflooring.com; Regency daybed in 'Zig Zag' fabric by Enid Marx, part of Borderline fabrics designer collection, distributed by www.rosebankfabrics.com; Gold Rubber side table by Fredrikson Stallard from David Gill Galleries; Florence Knoll Coffee Table by Knoll; George Smith Signature Sofa by George Smith, www.georgesmith.com; Tolomeo Floor Lamp by Artemide; Photograph by Anita Calero / Supervision New York; 606 Universal Shelving System designed by Dieter Rams for Vitsœ;

Blue Bedroom Spring lamp by Marianna Kennedy, www.mariannakennedy.com; Tolomeo Basculante Tavolo Table Lamp by Artemide; Drum Table by Paul Mayen for Habitat, www.habitat.co.uk; Pillow fabric 'Chou Chou Red' by Sister Parish; Quilt by Anthropologie; Haitian paintings from maret in Santo Domingo; Wingchair Manuel Canovas fabric by Colefax and Fowler.

Publishing Director Sarah Lavelle

Commissioning Editor Zena Alkayat

Editor Imogen Fortes

Head of Design Claire Rochford

Senior Designer Emily Lapworth

Photographer Sarah Hogan

Picture Research Samantha Rolfe-Hoang

Head of Production Stephen Lang

Production Controller Nikolaus Ginelli

Published in 2020 by Quadrille,
an imprint of Hardie Grant Publishing

Quadrille
52–54 Southwark Street
London SE1 1UN
quadrille.com

Cataloguing in Publication Data: a catalogue record
for this book is available from the British Library.

Text © Emilio Pimentel-Reid 2020
Photography © Sarah Hogan 2020
Design © Quadrille 2020

ISBN 9781787135116

Printed in China